Growing Daily *with* JESUS

Devotional

January - June

A Bible-based devotional for children and young people

Dr Cecilia OKOROCHUKWU

Growing Daily *with* JESUS

Devotional

January - June

A Bible-based devotional for children and young people

Fratee Media
Publishing | Web | Marketing

Growing Daily with Jesus Devotional: A Bible-based Devotional for Children and Young People
Copyright © 2024 Dr Cecilia Okorochukwu

@iamtdparent
www.deliberateparenting.com
info@deliberateparenting.com
www.youtube.com/@deliberateparentinghub

ISBN:
978-978-620-88-0-0 (eBook)
978-978-620-88-1-7 (Paperback)

Published in Nigeria by:
Fratee Media
28 Ezilo Avenue, Independence Layout,
Enugu, Enugu State, Nigeria.
www.fratee.com
hello@fratee.com
+234(0)8070701380

Cover & Layout Design by:
Fratee Graphics
fratee.com/graphics

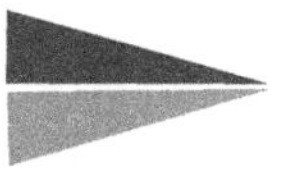 # Dedication

This Quiet Time devotional is dedicated to the following people:

To all the bright and curious children who open these pages, may your hearts be filled with wonder and your minds with wisdom as you journey through God's Word.

To my loving husband, whose support and encouragement have been my anchor.

To my precious children, whose smiles, questions and curiosity have inspired me to write this piece.

# Acknowledgements

Firstly, I give thanks to God Almighty for His guidance and inspiration throughout this journey.

My heartfelt appreciation goes to my family for their unwavering support and love. To my children, your curiosity and joy have been my motivation and inspiration. To my husband, thank you for your constant encouragement, understanding and support.

A special thanks to Fratee Media who edited, designed and published this piece. Thank you for your insightful edits and suggestions that helped shape this devotional.

I am also thankful to Valerie Ani who made wonderful contributions to this amazing devotional.

I am particularly grateful for the Sunday School Zone that provided the activities and puzzles used in writing this guide.

Lastly, I am grateful to the children and parents who will read this devotional. My hope and prayer are that it will bring you closer to Jesus and help you grow in your faith.

With love and gratitude,

Cecilia.
December, 2024.

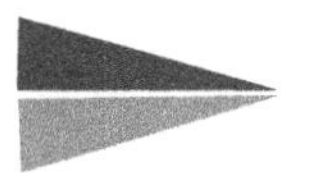

Contents

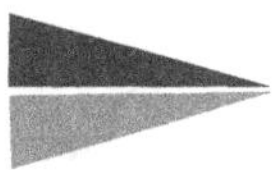# Introduction

Dear Young Friends,

Welcome to your very own Quiet Time Guide! This special book is designed to help you spend quality and meaningful time with God each day as your friend. Imagine having a daily adventure where you can explore God's love, wisdom, and amazing stories from the Bible. That's what this guide is all about!

Why Quiet Time?

Quiet time is like having a special meeting with your best friend. It's a moment set aside just for you and God. The following are why quiet time is important:

- **Know God Better:** When you read the Bible and pray, you learn more about who God is and how much He loves you.
- **Grow Spiritually:** Spending time with God helps you grow stronger in your faith, make wise choices, become a better you, and rule your world.
- **Feel God's Peace and Presence:** In the busy hustle and bustle of everyday life, quiet time gives you a chance to slow down, relax, and feel God's peaceful presence.

How to Use This Guide

Using this guide is easy and fun! Here's a step-by-step way to make the most of your quiet time:

1. **Find a Quiet Spot:** Choose a place

where you can sit quietly without distractions. It could be your bedroom, dining room, sitting room, or a cozy corner.

2. **Set a Time:** Decide on a regular time each day for your quiet time. It could be in the morning, afternoon, or evening—whatever works best for you. Most children prefer doing their quiet time before going to school or just after coming back from school.

3. **Follow the Daily Steps:**

   o **Bible Verse:** Start by reading the topic for the day and the Bible verse. This is a special message from God to you.

   o **Reflection:** Think about what the verse means. There will be a short explanation to help you understand.

    ○   **Prayer:** Talk to God. You can use the prayer provided or say your own.

    ○   **Action:** Do the fun activity to put into practice what you've learned. Yes, this book contains fun activities, I know you like to have fun.

What to Expect

Each day, you'll discover something new and exciting about God's Word. Here's what you'll find in your daily devotional:

- **A Daily Bible Verse:** A short, meaningful verse to read and memorise.
- **A Reflection:** Easy-to-understand thoughts that help explain the verse.

- **A Prayer:** A simple prayer to help you talk to God.
- **An Action:** A fun and practical activity to apply what you've learnt.

Tips for a Great Quiet Time

- **Be Consistent:** Try to have your quiet time at the same time every day. This helps you build a good habit.
- **Be Honest:** Talk to God about anything that's on your mind. How is your day going? Did anyone annoy you? He loves to hear from you!
- **Be Creative:** Use your imagination during your quiet time. Draw pictures, write in a journal, or sing songs of praise.

- **Listen to the Holy Spirit**: Allow Him to minister/talk to you.
- **Make Notes:** Jot down things that speak to you as you study and meditate. It will help both your spiritual life and well-being in general.

Join the Adventure

As you journey through this guide, remember that you are not alone. God is with you every step of the way just like He promised us in Joshua 1:9, and so are all the other children and young adults using this guide all over the world. Together, we are growing closer to God and learning to live out His love.

So, let's get started! Open your heart and mind to the wonderful things God has in store for you. This is going to be an amazing adventure, and I'm excited to walk this path with you.

With love and blessings,
Cecilia.

January

The Creation Story/Fall of Man

Introduction

This month, we are going to be looking at the creation of the universe. Long ago, before there were stars in the beautiful sky or green grass on the ground, the world was like a blank canvas waiting for a touch of beauty.

In this emptiness, God called the Trinity and said let us make the world a beautiful place to live. God decided to create everything wonderful, and so He began to create.

Every human being and animal on earth was made by God. We are no accidents on earth, God made us to have dominion over the other things He has created.

Day 1: In the Beginning
Scripture: Genesis 1:1

Story: God created the heavens and the earth.

While heaven is God's throne, earth is His footstool, symbolizing His presence in both realms. The earth is the place where humans live, work, and experience God's creation. It is also the stage for the unfolding story of God's relationship with humanity.

Lesson: God is the Creator of everything.
Reflection: How does it feel to know that God made everything?
Prayer: Thank You Lord for creating the world and everything in it.
Action: Draw a picture of what you imagine the world like when God first created it.

Day 2: Let There Be Light
Scripture: Genesis 1:3–4

Story: God creates light and separates it from darkness.

Why is light important? Light is incredibly important, and it plays a vital role in our world. Light gives **Life and Growth.** Light, especially sunlight, is crucial for the growth of plants through a process called photosynthesis. **Light gives us vision.**

Lesson: God brings light into our lives.
Reflection: How can you let God's light shine in your life?
Prayer: God, help me to shine Your light.
Action: Make a light switch cover with the words "Let there be light" to remind you of God's creation.

Day 3: The Sky
Scripture: Genesis 1:6–8

Story: God creates the sky.
The sky is a lovely place and is beautiful to behold. The sky is a vast, ever-changing canvas that stretches above us. During the day, it can be brilliant blue, clear, and bright, with the sun shining down and casting warmth and light.

Lesson: God's creation is vast and wonderful.
Reflection: What do you think about when you look at the sky?
Prayer: God, thank You for the beautiful sky and all of Your creation. Amen.
Action: Spend some time outside looking at the sky and thanking God for His creation.

Day 4: The Land and Seas
Scripture: Genesis 1:9–10

Story: God creates dry land and gathers the waters.

God created the waters. Water flows down the mountains, turning into swift, gurgling streams that sing as they dance over rocks and pebbles. Plants and trees flourish along the riverbanks, creating lush forests teeming with life. We get our food from the plants nourished by water.

Lesson: God's creation is perfectly ordered.
Reflection: How can you see God's order in creation?
Prayer: Father, thank You for creating the land and seas. Help us to take care of them.
Action: Draw a picture of the land and seas.

Day 5: Plants and Trees
Scripture: Genesis 1:11–12

Story: God creates plants and trees.
God created plants and trees which reflect His wisdom, creativity and provision.
Food and Sustenance: Plants and trees are a primary source of food for both humans and animals. They provide fruits, vegetables, and other edible parts that sustain life. Can you live and survive without food for days/months/years?

Lesson: God provides food and beauty through His creation.
Reflection: What is your favourite food and why?
Prayer: God, thank You for the plants and trees that give us food and beauty.
Action: Plant a seed and care for it.

Day 6: Sun, Moon, and Stars
Scripture: Genesis 1:14–19

Story: God creates the sun, moon, and stars to give light and mark time.
The moon and stars are among the most enchanting sights in the night sky, each holding a unique beauty and wonder.
The Moon: The moon has a serene and captivating presence.
The Stars: The stars are like tiny sparkling jewels scattered across the vast canvas of the sky.

Lesson: God created the heavenly bodies to guide us.
Prayer: Thank You, God, for the sun, moon, and stars that guide and light our way. Amen.
Action: Draw the sun, moon, and stars.

Day 7: Birds and Sea Creatures
Scripture: Genesis 1:20–23

Story: God creates birds to fly and creatures to fill the seas.

God also created birds of every kind to soar through the sky. Brightly coloured parrots, swift eagles, gentle doves, and cheerful songbirds all began to fly and fill the air with their beautiful songs.

Lesson: God's creation is diverse and wonderful.

Reflection: What is your favourite bird or sea creature, and why?

Prayer: Lord, thank You for the amazing birds and sea creatures You created. Amen.

Action: Draw and colour a picture of your favourite bird or sea creature.

Day 8: Land Animals
Scripture: Genesis 1:24–25

Story: God creates animals to fill the earth. This story reminds us of the beauty and diversity of life in the seas and the skies, and how everything is part of God's amazing creation. These animals help us produce food, clothes, and many other things like manure, making the soil rich and fertile.

Lesson: God's creation is full of life and variety.

Reflection: What is your favourite land animal, and why?

Prayer: God, thank You for creating all the animals. Help us to care for them.

Action: Visit a zoo or farm, or draw your favourite land animal.

Day 9: Creation of Man
Scripture: Genesis 1:26–27

Story: God creates man and woman in His image.

God wanted to make a being in His own image, someone who could think, feel, and take care of His wonderful creations. God made man from the dust. He breathed into the man's nostrils the breath of life and named him Adam.

Lesson: We are made in the image of God.

Reflection: What does it mean for you to be made in God's image?

Prayer: Dear God, thank You for creating us in Your image.

Action: Make a self-portrait and write "Made in God's image" on it.

Day 10: God Rested on the 7th Day
Scripture: Genesis 2:1–3

Story: God rests on the seventh day.
Rest is a beautiful thing. Our body needs rest. We should not always play and get busy with social media or cartoons. When we rest, our body recuperates and functions better.

Lesson: Rest is important and holy.
Reflection: How can you take time to rest and appreciate God's creation?
Prayer: Lord, thank You for showing us the importance of rest. Help us to rest in You. Amen.
Action: Spend a quiet time in nature, resting and reflecting on God's creation.

Day 11: The Garden of Eden
Scripture: Genesis 2:8–9

Story: God creates a beautiful garden for man to live in.

God placed Adam in a beautiful garden called the Garden of Eden. This garden was filled with all kinds of trees and plants that were pleasing to the eye and good for food. In the middle of the garden, God placed the Tree of Life and the Tree of the Knowledge of Good and Evil.

Lesson: God provides everything we need.
Reflection: How does it feel to know that God provides for you?
Prayer: Thank You, God, for providing for all our needs. Amen.
Action: Create a mini garden using small plants or drawings.

Day 12: Adam Names the Animals
Scripture: Genesis 2:19–20

Story: Adam names the animals God created.

God gave Adam the responsibility to take care of the garden and the animals. He also gave Adam the freedom to eat from any tree in the garden, except for the Tree of the Knowledge of Good and Evil.

Lesson: God gave us the responsibility to care for His creation.

Reflection: How can you help take care of God's creation?

Prayer: Lord, help us to be responsible caretakers of Your creation. Amen.

Action: Make a list of ways you can help care for animals and the environment.

Day 13: The Creation of Eve
Scripture: Genesis 2:21–23

Story: God creates Eve as a companion for Adam.

God saw that it was not good for Adam to be alone, so He decided to make a companion for him. God took one of Adam's ribs and used it to create a woman. God brought the woman to Adam and Adam was excited. He named her Eve.

Lesson: God created us for relationships.

Reflection: How can you show love and care to the people in your life?

Prayer: God, thank You for creating us for relationships.

Action: Do something kind for a friend or family member.

Day 14: Life in the Garden
Scripture: Genesis 2:15

Story: God places Adam and Eve in the Garden of Eden to care for it.
God made the garden beautiful, they had everything they needed. The things God made created shapes and patterns that spark the imagination. Is God not awesome, wise, and loving?

Lesson: We are stewards of God's creation.
Reflection: How can you be a good steward of what God has given you?
Prayer: Lord, help me to take care of the world You have entrusted to us.
Action: Pick up a litter to take care of your environment.

Day 15: The Tree of Knowledge
Scripture: Genesis 2:16–17

Story: God commands Adam and Eve not to eat from the tree of knowledge.
God commanded them not to eat that fruit. Now you might ask, why did God create the tree? It might be because God has given man options but advised him to make wise choices.

Lesson: Obedience to God is important.
Reflection: Why is it important to obey God's commands?
Prayer: God, help us to obey Your commands and trust in Your wisdom. Amen.
Action: Write down some of God's commands that you want to remember and follow.

Day 16: The Temptation
Scripture: Genesis 3:1–5

Story: The serpent tempts Eve to eat from the tree of knowledge.

In the beautiful Garden of Eden, Adam and Eve lived happily, enjoying the lush surroundings and the company of all the animals. They had everything they could possibly need and spent their days taking care of the garden.

Lesson: Temptation can lead us away from God.

Reflection: How can you resist temptation in your life?

Prayer: Lord, help us to resist temptation and stay close to You.

Action: Talk with a parent or guardian about ways to resist temptation.

Day 17: The Fall of Man
Scripture: Genesis 3:6–7

Story: Adam and Eve ate the forbidden fruit.

A cunning serpent enticed Eve to disobey God, she ate and gave it to Adam. This story helps us understand the importance of obeying God, and it shows that even when we make mistakes, God still loves us. Despite our mistakes, we should still ask God for forgiveness.

Lesson: Sin separates us from God.
Reflection: How does sin affect our relationship with God?
Prayer: God, help us to stay close to You.
Action: Write a prayer asking for forgiveness for a specific sin.

Day 18: God's Question
Scripture: Genesis 3:8–9

Story: God asks Adam and Eve where they are after they hide.
Ask yourself, am I hiding? Just like when we do bad things like taking sweets that are not ours, we panic and try to hide from Mum and Dad. We cannot hide from God.

Lesson: God seeks us out even when we hide from Him.
Reflection: How does it feel to know that God seeks you out?
Prayer: Thank you Lord for seeking us out and loving us even when we sin.
Action: Draw a picture of Adam and Eve hiding and God looking for them.

Day 19: The Blame Game
Scripture: Genesis 3:12–13

Story: Adam and Eve blame each other and the serpent for their sin.
When we sin either by omission or commission, we should admit and accept that we have sinned and ask God for forgiveness and not try to find who or what to blame.

Lesson: We should take responsibility for our actions.
Reflection: Why is it important to take responsibility for our mistakes?
Prayer: Lord, help us to take responsibility for our actions and seek forgiveness. Amen.
Action: Think of a time when you made a mistake and apologised for it.

Day 20: The Consequences
Scripture: Genesis 3:16–19

Story: God tells Adam and Eve the consequences of their sin.

God told the serpent that it would be cursed and would have to crawl on its belly and eat dust all the days of its life. Eve would experience pain in childbirth, and Adam would till the ground and work hard to produce food.

Lesson: Sin has consequences.

Reflection: How does it feel to know that God loves you even when you sin?

Prayer: God, thank You for loving us even when we make mistakes.

Action: Write down a way you can make better choices in the future.

Day 21: Reflection

If you were Adam, what would you have done?
If you were Eve, what would you have done?
If they did not sin, what would have happened?
Reason and discuss with your family/friends.

A possible answer:
If I Were Adam or Eve
If I were Adam or Eve, knowing what I know, I would have tried to resist the temptation to eat the forbidden fruit. It's a tough scenario because the serpent was very persuasive, and the desire for wisdom and the knowledge of good and evil was strong. However, obedience to God and trusting His plan would have been my priority.

Day 22: Leaving the Garden
Scripture: Genesis 3:22–23

Story: Adam and Eve were sent out of the Garden of Eden.

The consequence was for Adam and Eve to leave the garden and experience the results of their action — suffering. When we do bad things like lying, stealing, etc, we leave God's presence and become vulnerable to the enemy. That's why we should always ask God to forgive us when we sin.

Reflection: How can you still feel close to God even when you face difficulties?

Prayer: Help me, God, to stay close to You no matter what.

Action: Write a letter to God about your feelings.

Day 23: Life Outside the Garden

Story: Adam and Eve had to work hard and face challenges.

Adam suffered to get food and other provisions for his family because the ground was cursed. Eve also suffered in childbirth. They lost divine provisions and the easy life God had provided for them from the beginning. Now man also has to battle to overcome sin on a daily basis just because Adam and Eve failed God

Reflection: How do challenges help us grow stronger?

Prayer: God, give me the strength to face my challenges.

Action: Do a chore or task that helps you understand hard work.

Day 24: God's Provision
Scripture: Genesis 2:8–9

"Now the Lord God had planted a garden in the east, in Eden; and there he put the man he had formed. The Lord God made all kinds of trees grow out of the ground — trees that were pleasing to the eye and good for food."

Story: God provided clothes for Adam and Eve.

Despite our sins, God still loves us and provides for us.

Reflection: How does God provide for us today?

Prayer: Thank you, God, for always taking care of us.

Action: Make a list of things you are thankful for that God has provided.

Day 25: God's Presence
Scripture: Genesis 3:8

Story: God was still with Adam and Eve after they sinned against Him.

This is because of the unconditional love He has for man. We need God's presence in our lives to worship and adore Him and get the power to overcome the devil and his schemes. Without God's presence, we will be prey to the enemy. Even in your school, ask God for His Presence.

Reflection: How does it feel to know that God never leaves us?

Prayer: Thank you, God, for always being with us.

Action: Spend time in prayer, thanking God for His presence.

Day 26: God's Love
Scripture: Isaiah 43:3

Story: God continued to love Adam and Eve.

Despite the fall of man, God still loved us and made an alternative plan to redeem us through Jesus Christ. He wants us to appreciate this love by loving Him back and living as Christ's ambassadors.

Reflection: How does God's love help us even when we make mistakes?

Prayer: Thank you, God, for Your unconditional love.

Action: Show love to someone today by doing something kind for them.

Day 27: God's Plan
Scripture: Jeremiah 29:11

Story: God had a plan to redeem humanity through Jesus.
Every good thing or project requires planning. God's ultimate plan for salvation and redemption through Jesus Christ is what made Jesus die to redeem us. Understanding God's plan helps believers to trust in His wisdom, even when life's circumstances are challenging.

Reflection: How does it feel to know that God has a plan for us?
Prayer: Thank you, God, for Your plan to save us.
Action: Write or draw about what you think God's plan for you might be.

Day 28: Learning from the Fall
Scripture: Genesis 3:12–13

Story: Adam and Eve's story teaches us about sin and redemption.

For us to understand this, we need to identify common temptations we face and find practical ways to avoid or overcome them, such as prayer, accountability, and immersing ourselves in God's word. We should take responsibility for our actions. Reflect on situations where you might have shifted blame. Practice taking responsibility for your actions and seek forgiveness when necessary.

Reflection: What can we learn from Adam and Eve's story?

Prayer: God, help me to make wise choices and take responsibility for my actions.

Day 29: Enticement
Scripture: Proverbs 1:10

What is enticement? **Enticement** means the act of attracting or tempting someone to do something, often by offering something desirable or appealing. This concept can have both positive and negative connotations depending on the context.

Positive enticement can involve encouraging someone to do something beneficial or enjoyable, e.g., doing homework, or doing house chores.

The negative enticement is when it leads to sin. If a friend or someone entices you with money or food or anything and asks you to sin against God, what would you do?

Action/steps to take to say NO to sin:

1. Say no politely.
2. Run away.
3. Tell a trusted adult.

Day 30:
Scripture: Psalm 1:1–3

We should delight our hearts in God, meditate on His word, and keep good company so that we will not fall into sin. Even if we fall by omission or commission, we should be remorseful and ask God to forgive us. Think of how you as a good friend can help your friend come out of sin or say no to evil enticement or temptations. What actions/steps would you tell your friend to take?

Actions could be:
1. Pray for God to change their hearts.
2. Preach to them.
3. Live an exemplary life for them to copy you.

Day 31: Complete the puzzle below

Notes

February
Salvation

Introduction

This month we will be looking at salvation.
Let us look at the story of Zacchaeus as a case study.
Scripture: Luke 19:1–10

Story: Zacchaeus was a chief tax collector and very wealthy, but he was also disliked by many because tax collectors often cheated people. Zacchaeus was curious about Jesus, so when Jesus came to his town, Zacchaeus climbed a tree to see Him because he was short and couldn't see over the crowd.

When Jesus saw Zacchaeus, He called him by name and told him to come down because He wanted to stay at his house.

The people were surprised and even upset because they thought Zacchaeus was a sinner and unworthy of Jesus' attention.

Despite what others thought, Jesus showed kindness to Zacchaeus. This act of love and acceptance changed Zacchaeus' heart. He promised to give half of his wealth to the poor and repay anyone he had cheated four times the amount. Jesus declared that salvation had come to Zacchaeus' house, for he had become a true child of Abraham, showing that even those who are lost can be saved when they encounter Jesus.

Day 1: What is Salvation?
Scripture: Luke 19:1–10

Salvation is being saved from sin and its consequences, and being brought into a right relationship with God. It's a central theme of Christianity, showcasing God's love and mercy towards humanity. Salvation involves recognising our wrongdoings, repenting, and turning our lives towards God, just like Zacchaeus.

Lesson: Salvation is a gift from God.

Reflection: Think about a time when you felt far from God.

Prayer: Dear Jesus, thank You for Your amazing love and offering us salvation.

Action: Share the story of Zacchaeus with a friend/family member, talk about how Jesus' love can change lives.

Day 2: God Loves us and gave His son Jesus
Scripture: John 3:16

After Adam and Eve failed God, God has been reconciling man back to Himself. In the New Testament, God gave us His only son Jesus to die on the cross and save us from sin.

Lesson: God loves us so much that He gave His Son, Jesus, so we can have eternal life.

Reflection: Think about how much God loves you.

Prayer: Father, thank You for loving me and sending Jesus to save me.

Action: Draw a picture of a cross and write "God loves me" on it.

Day 3: Why Do We Need Salvation?
Scripture: Romans 3:23

To sin means to do something that goes against God's teachings or moral laws. Imagine you have a set of rules that help everyone get along better. In a similar way, God has given us rules to live by—the Bible. Sin can hurt our relationship with God and others because it usually involves doing something wrong like lying, stealing, etc.

Lesson: We all have sinned and fallen short of God's glory.
Prayer: Lord, please forgive me and help me to follow You.
Action: Write down one thing you need to ask God to forgive you for.

Day 4: Jesus, Our Saviour
Scripture: Matthew 1:21

We as Christian children believe that Jesus came into the world to save us from our sins and its consequences, offering eternal life through His sacrifice on the cross and subsequent resurrection. This is the central truth of the Christian faith.

Lesson: Jesus came to save His people from their sins.

Reflection: How and why did Jesus save us? By dying on the Cross, the reason is to reconcile us back to God.

Prayer: Thank You, Jesus, for coming to save me from my sins.

Action: Write a thank-you note to Jesus and keep it in a place where you can easily see it daily.

Day 5: The Good News
Scripture: Mark 16:15

Called "Good News" because it brings a message of hope, salvation, and God's love for humanity. **It means the following:**

1. **God's Love**: God loves the world He created and every person in it.
2. **Jesus' Sacrifice**: Because of sin, our relationship with God was broken. But God sent His Son, Jesus Christ to save us from our sins.

Lesson: We are called to share the good news of Jesus.

Reflection: Who can you tell about Jesus today?

Prayer: God, help us to share the good news of Jesus with others.

Action: Tell a friend/family member about Jesus.

Day 6: Repentance
Scripture: Acts 3:19

What is Repentance? Repentance is a heartfelt and sincere turning away from sin and turning towards God.

1. Recognition: Realising that you have done something wrong or that you have sinned.

2. Regret: Confess your sin, and make amendments.

Repentance is not just about feeling sorry; it's about making a real change in your heart and actions. It's a way to restore your relationship with God and live in a way that pleases God.

Reflection: What is something you need to repent from?

Prayer: Lord, help us to repent from our sins and turn to You. Amen.

Action: Write a prayer of repentance in your journal.

Day 7: Faith in Jesus
Scripture: Ephesians 2:8

For us to accept Jesus as our Lord and personal Saviour, we first need to believe in Jesus and have faith in Him. When we believe in Him, He makes us His children. Without faith, we cannot come to Jesus. Make up your mind to follow Him.

Lesson: We are saved by grace through faith.

Reflection: What does it mean to have faith in Jesus?

Prayer: Dear Jesus, help us to have faith in You and trust You completely. Amen.

Action: Write down what you believe about Jesus.

Day 8: Being Born Again
Scripture: John 3:3

In this verse, Jesus explained to Nicodemus that he must be born of Water and the Spirit. This means accepting the word of God which is like water that cleanses, receiving the Holy Spirit, and undergoing a spiritual rebirth.

Lesson: Jesus said we must be born again to see the kingdom of God.

Reflection: What does it mean to be born again?

Prayer: Father, thank You for giving us new life in You.

Action: Draw a picture of something depicting a new life, like a butterfly or a flower.

Day 9: God's Grace
Scripture: Ephesians 2:8–9

Story: Jesus came to earth to show us the way back to God.

Because of Jesus' sacrifice, God offers us a free gift — salvation. It's like a wonderful surprise! We don't have to earn it or work for it. All we need to do is believe in Jesus and trust in Him.

Lesson: Salvation is a gift from God, not something we can earn.

Reflection: How do you feel knowing that salvation is a gift?

Prayer: Thank You, God, for Your amazing grace. Amen.

Action: Make a salvation gratitude card and keep it in your room near your bed.

Day 10: Assurance of Salvation
Scripture: 1 John 5:13

It is a blessed assurance that Jesus died for me.

Lesson: We can be sure of our salvation in Jesus.

Reflection: How does it feel to know you are saved?

Prayer: God, thank You for the assurance of salvation through Jesus.

Action: Write down what it means to be sure of your salvation.

Song

Blessed assurance, Jesus is mine
O what a foretaste of glory divine
Heir of salvation, purchase of God
I'm born of His Spirit, washed in His blood

This is my story, this is my song
Praising my Saviour all the day long (repeat)

Day 11: Walking in the Light
Scripture: 1 John 1:7

Walking in the light as a Christian refers to living a life of righteousness, honesty, and transparency according to God's principles. It involves following Jesus Christ, who is described as the Light of the world, and living in accordance with His teachings.

Lesson: Walk in the light as Jesus is in the light.

Reflection: What does it mean to walk in the light?

Prayer: Lord, help us to walk in Your light every day. Amen.

Action: Draw a picture of a path with light shining on it.

Day 12: New Creation
Scripture: 2 Corinthians 5:17

Spiritual Rebirth: When a person accepts Jesus, they are spiritually reborn. This means that their old, sinful nature is replaced by a new, righteous nature.

Forgiveness of Sins: Through faith in Jesus, a person's sins are forgiven.

Indwelling of the Holy Spirit, Transformation: The new creation involves a transformation in the way a person thinks, acts, and lives.

Lesson: In Christ, we are new creations.

Reflection: How has Jesus made you new?

Prayer: Thank You, Jesus, for making us new creations in You.

Action: Write down ways you have changed since knowing Jesus.

Day 13: The Holy Spirit
Scripture: Acts 2:38

Without the Holy Spirit we cannot obey God, The Holy Spirit helps us live for Jesus. He is our Comforter and Helper and gives us the strength to keep our salvation. We will study more on the Holy Spirit in the month of May (You can read it today as well).

Lesson: The Holy Spirit is given to those who believe in Jesus.

Reflection: How does the Holy Spirit help you?

Prayer: Holy Spirit, thank You for being with us and guiding us. Amen.

Action: Draw a picture representing the Holy Spirit, like a dove or flames.

Day 14: Living for Jesus
Scripture: Galatians 2:20

God's love is always with us, no matter where we go or what we do. It's like having a best friend who never leaves your side. God is Omnipresent.

Giving and Generous: God gave us His Dear son Jesus and has also given us many wonderful things, like our family, friends, and everything around us.

Lesson: Our old self is crucified with Christ, and we now live for Jesus.

Reflection: How can you live for Jesus every day?

Prayer: Jesus, help us to live our lives for You.

Action: Write down ways you can live for Jesus.

Day 15: God's Love
Scripture: Romans 5:8

God's Amazing Love

Imagine the most wonderful, warm, and comforting hug you've ever had. That's a little bit like how God's love feels. It's a love that's bigger and more powerful than anything you can imagine.

Unconditional Love: God's love is unconditional, which means He loves us no matter what. He is **Caring, Protective, and Forgiving.**

Lesson: God shows His love for us by sending Jesus to die for us.

Reflection: How does God's love make you feel?

Prayer: Thank You, God, for Your incredible love for us.

Action: Draw a heart and write "God loves me" inside.

Day 16: Eternal Life
Scripture: John 3:16

Jesus has promised us everlasting life with Him when we accept Him and walk in His ways. He has gone to heaven to prepare beautiful mansions for each of us. Are you preparing to meet Jesus? How ready are you? Jesus is coming soon.

Lesson: Believing in Jesus gives us eternal life.

Reflection: What do you think eternal life with Jesus will be like?

Prayer: Thank You, Jesus, for the gift of eternal life. Amen.

Action: Draw a picture of what you imagine heaven to be like.

Day 17: The Great Commission
Scripture: Matthew 28:19–20

As we are saved, Jesus wants us to preach to others to get saved. We can do this by verbally preaching to them, and sharing the word of God through social media platforms like WhatsApp, Snapchat, Tiktok, Twitter, Facebook, etc. This is essential because we would want our friends and families in Heaven with us.

Lesson: Jesus calls us to make disciples of all nations.

Reflection: How can you help others learn about Jesus?

Prayer: Lord, help us to share Your love and make disciples. Amen.

Action: Share a Bible story with a friend, sibling, or neighbour.

Day 18: God's Word
Scripture: Psalm 119:105

Once upon a time, a boy lost his way home from school. He read the map and found his way back home, his heart filled with peace. God's word is our map for living victorious lives. It lightens the way and guides us.

Lesson: God's Word is a lamp to our feet and a light to our path.
Reflection: How can the Bible guide you each day?
Prayer: Thank You, God, for giving us Your Word to guide us. Amen.
Action: Write down steps you would take when you are lost or when you sin against God.

Day 19: Faith and Works
Scripture: James 2:17

We need to put our Faith to work.

Why do we need Faith?

Hope and Assurance: Faith provides hope and assurance, especially during difficult times. **Guidance**: Faith in God gives us direction and purpose in life.

Strength and Resilience, Comfort and Peace: Faith brings a sense of peace and comfort, knowing that we are loved and cared for by a higher power.

Lesson: Faith without works is dead.

Reflection: How can your actions show your faith?

Prayer: God, help us to show our faith through our actions.

Action: Do a good deed for someone in need.

Day 20: God's Plan
Scripture: Jeremiah 29:11

God has a divine plan for each of us and for the world. God created the world and everything in it out of love. As children we need to ask Him to guide us into His plans for us. We should depend and rely on His plans because He knows us more than we know ourselves.

Lesson: God has a plan and a purpose for each of us.

Reflection: What do you think God's plan for you is?

Prayer: Lord, thank You for having a wonderful plan for our lives.

Action: Make a timetable for your daily activities.

Day 21: Jesus is the Bread of Life
Scripture: John 6:35

What does 'Jesus is the bread of Life' mean? It means:

1. Spiritual Nourishment: Just as bread nourishes our physical bodies, Jesus nourishes our souls; He provides us with spiritual strength and fulfillment.

2. Daily Dependence: Just as we eat bread as food, this keeps our faith strong and our hearts aligned with God.

Lesson: Jesus is the Bread of Life who satisfies our spiritual hunger.

Reflection: How does Jesus satisfy your soul?

Prayer: Jesus, thank You for being the Bread of Life.

Action: Share a snack with someone and talk about how Jesus is the Bread of Life.

Day 22: Jesus the Good Shepherd
Scripture: John 10:11

A shepherd is someone who takes care of sheep, guiding them to safe pastures, protecting them from harm, and ensuring they are healthy and well-fed.

Shepherds do the following:

1. Guiding the Flock: A shepherd leads the sheep to places where they can find good grass to eat and clean water to drink.

2. Protecting from Danger, Caring for Their Needs

Lesson: Jesus is the Good Shepherd who cares for His sheep

Reflection: How does Jesus take care of you?

Prayer: Thank You, Jesus, for being our Good Shepherd.

Action: Draw a picture of Jesus as the Good Shepherd.

Day 23: The Way, the Truth, and the Life
Scripture: John 14:6

There are many ways to different destinations, but Jesus is the ONLY way to God. Some children believe through other routes, they can get to God, but this is wrong. Jesus is the ONLY way to God.

Lesson: Jesus is the way, the truth, and the life.

Reflection: What does it mean that Jesus is the way, the truth, and the life?

Prayer: Jesus, thank You for being the way, the truth, and the life.

Action: Write down what it means to you that Jesus is the way, the truth, and the life.

Day 24: Jesus, the Light of the World
Scripture: John 8:12

Jesus as the Light of the world: Just as light shows us the way in the dark, Jesus provides guidance and direction in our lives. He helps us see the right path to take and make good choices.

Hope and Joy: Light brings hope and joy into our lives.

Lesson: Jesus is the light of the world, and we should follow Him.

Reflection: How can you follow Jesus' light?

Prayer: Thank You, Jesus, for being the Light of the world. Amen.

Action: Draw a candle with a flame to remind you that Jesus is the Light.

Day 25: Jesus, the Living Water
Scripture: John 4:14

You would agree with me that we need water daily. Water is incredibly important for many reasons. It is essential for life and plays a crucial role in our daily lives and the environment. When we come to Jesus, He satisfies our soul, just like He did for the Samaritan woman.

Lesson: As we cannot live and survive without water, likewise, we cannot survive without Jesus because He is the water of life.

Prayer: Oh Lord, help me to always long for you, just as the deer longs for water.

Activity: Draw a deer drinking water from a bowl.

Day 26

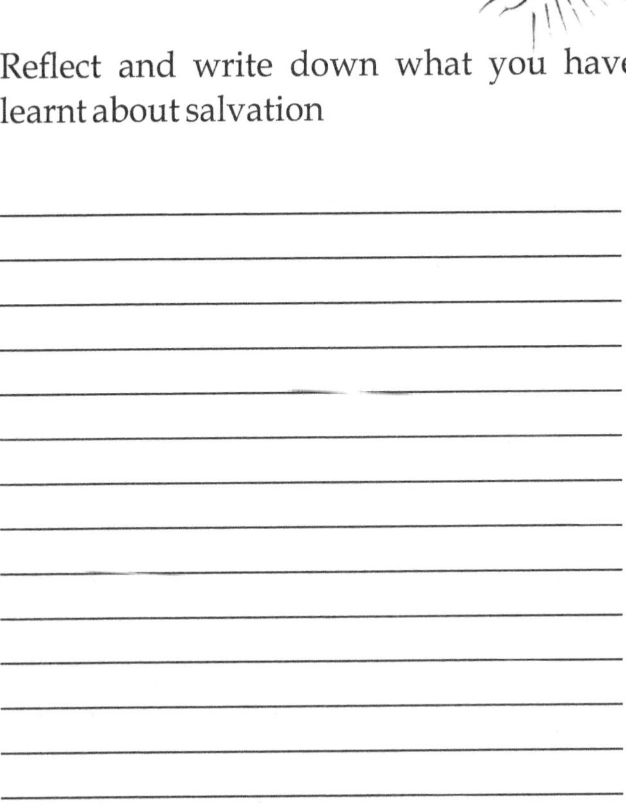

Reflect and write down what you have learnt about salvation

____

____

____

____

____

____

____

____

____

____

____

____

Day 27

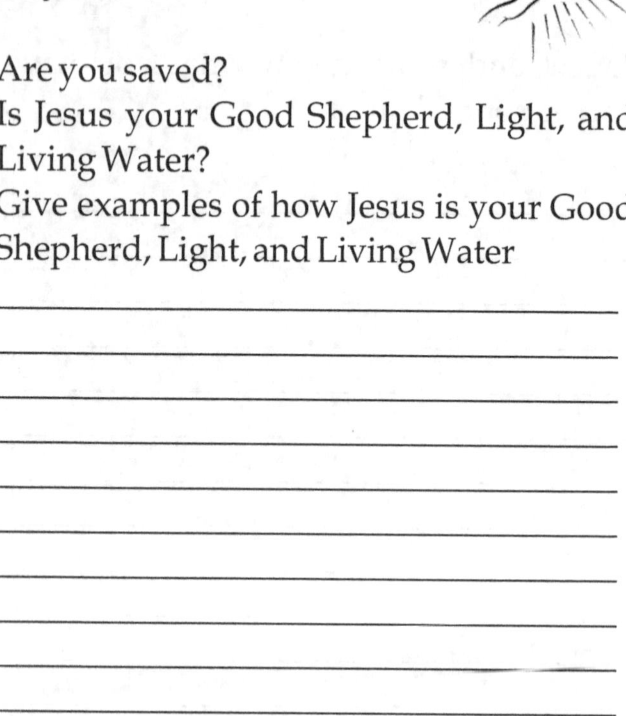

Are you saved?
Is Jesus your Good Shepherd, Light, and Living Water?
Give examples of how Jesus is your Good Shepherd, Light, and Living Water

____

____

____

____

____

____

____

____

____

____

Day 28: Solve the puzzle on Salvation

Helmet of Salvation Connect the Dots

Connect the dots to complete the helmet.

Notes

MARCH

March

Disciple-ship

Introduction

Being a disciple of Jesus means following Him and learning from Him. It also means sharing His love and teachings with others. We can be "fishers of people" by showing kindness, helping others, and talking about Jesus.

Day 1: Following Jesus
Scripture: Matthew 4:19

Story: Jesus called His first disciples, Peter and Andrew, while they were fishing. He invited them to follow Him and promised to make them "fishers of men." They left their nets and followed Jesus.

Prayer: Dear Jesus, thank You for inviting us to follow You.

Activity: Create a paper fish craft and write one way you can show Jesus' love to others. Hang it up as a reminder to be a disciple of Jesus.

Reflection: Who are the people in your life that you can show Jesus' love today?

Action: Write how you can be a disciple.

Day 2: Jesus Calls His First Disciples
Scripture: Matthew 4:18–20

Summary: Jesus calls Peter and Andrew to follow Him.

Even Jesus is calling you today to be His Disciple and follow Him. Drop all your excuses.

Lesson: Jesus invites us to be His followers.

Prayer: Dear Jesus, help me to follow You every day. Amen.

Activity/Song:

I will make you fishers of men
Fishers of men 3x
I will make you fishers of men if you follow me
If you follow me 2x
I will make you fishers of men
If you follow me

Day 3: Jesus Calls Matthew
Scripture: Matthew 9:9

Story: Jesus calls Matthew, a tax collector, to follow Him.

Matthew, also known as Levi, was one of the disciples. Before becoming a disciple, he worked as a tax collector. Tax collectors were not nice, people did not want to associate with them but Jesus did not discriminate. Matthew obeyed Jesus when Jesus called him. Will you follow Jesus today?

Lesson: Jesus calls everyone, no matter who they are.

Prayer: Jesus, thank You for calling us to be Your disciples.

Activity: Make name tags and talk about how Jesus knows each of us by name.

Day 4: The Cost of Following Jesus
Scripture: Luke 9:23

Summary: Jesus teaches about the cost of being His disciple. He explained to them that they must make up their minds to follow Him. Deny ourselves and take up our cross.

Denying ourselves means not doing what our sinful nature wants.

Taking up our Cross means we would face opposition or mockery from unbelievers, but we should not give up. Stay committed by praying daily, reading the Bible, evangelising, etc.

Lesson: Following Jesus requires commitment.

Prayer: Jesus, help us to stay committed to following You.

Activity: Talk about ways we can be committed to Jesus.

Day 5: Peter's Faith
Scripture: Matthew 14:28–31

Summary: Peter walks on water but begins to sink when he doubts.

Initially, Peter had faith. As long as Peter looked unto Jesus, he walked on the water. But when he took his eyes off Jesus, he started sinking. We need to continually look unto Jesus so that we will not fall or derail. When doubt comes to our minds, we should pray to God to increase our faith.

Lesson: Trust in Jesus even when it's hard.
Prayer: Lord, help us to trust You always. Amen.
Activity: Make a paper boat, and talk about trusting Jesus.

Day 6: The Great Commission
Scripture: Matthew 28:19–20

Summary: Jesus commands His disciples to make more disciples.

Here is an explanation of the Great Commission. Jesus declared that all authority in heaven and on earth has been given to Him. **Go and Make Disciples, Baptising, and Teaching.**

The reason Jesus came to die on the cross is to save the world, we need to spread the Gospel of Jesus Christ to everyone.

Lesson: Jesus wants us to tell others about Him.

Prayer: Jesus, help us to share Your good news.

Activity: Make a "Great Commission" poster or drawing to remind us to tell others about Jesus.

Day 7: The Vine and the Branches
Scripture: John 15:5

Story: Jesus is the vine, and we are the branches.

A vine is a plant that has a unique way of growing. Instead of standing upright on its own, a vine relies on other structures to support its growth. As the leaves and stem of a tree cannot survive outside the tree/root, likewise we cannot survive in our Christian journey outside Jesus.

Lesson: We need to stay connected to Jesus.

Prayer: Lord, help us to stay close to You. Amen.

Activity: Draw a vine with branches and write ways we can stay connected to Jesus.

Day 8: Salt and Light
Scripture: Matthew 5:13–16

Summary: Jesus says we are the salt of the earth and the light of the world.

Have you ever eaten food cooked without salt? How was the taste? Awful right? Salt is essential to make the food tasty and yummy. As we cannot eat rice or pasta without salt, likewise Jesus wants us to be salt to the world. When there is light, darkness disappears.

Lesson: Shine Jesus' light through our actions.

Prayer: Jesus, help us to be salt and light in the world.

Song:
This little light of mine
I'm gonna let it shine 3x

Day 9: The Beatitudes
Scripture: Matthew 5:1–12

Story: Jesus teaches about blessings.

After Jesus fasted and prayed for 40 days and nights, He started by teaching the basics of Christian living, meaning Blessings.

Purpose of the Beatitudes:

1. Kingdom Values: Jesus used the Beatitudes to outline the values and characteristics that are esteemed in the Kingdom of God.

2. Encouragement and Spiritual Depth: They emphasise inner qualities like humility, mercy, purity of heart, and a hunger for righteousness.

3. Invitation to Transformation

Lesson: Jesus' teachings show us how to live blessed lives.

Prayer: Lord, help us to live according to Your Beatitudes.

Activity: Create a "Beatitudes" bookmark with key points.

Day 10: The Lord's Prayer
Scripture: Matthew 6:9–13

Summary: Jesus teaches His disciples how to pray.

Jesus knew that the disciples needed to learn how to pray, so He taught them. We are to use this pattern when we pray to God. Give thanks to God, pray for our needs, and forgive others. Each day, say the Lord's prayer. Pray is important; that is how we communicate with God.

Lesson: Prayer is talking to God.

Prayer: Our Father in heaven, hallowed be Your name… (Say the Lord's prayer together).

Activity: Learn our Lord's prayer, and recite it as much as can.

Day 11: Love One Another
Scripture: John 13:34–35

Summary: Jesus commands us to love one another.

God is love. If we do not love our neighbor, then we are not Christians.

If someone does what is bad to you, the normal reaction is to retaliate. But Jesus admonishes us to love the person, hate the sin or bad thing the person does, and then pray for the person to change and repent from the bad thing.

Lesson: Love shows we are Jesus' disciples.
Prayer: Jesus, help us to love others as You love us.
Activity: Make "love" cards and give them to friends or family.

Day 12: The Good Samaritan
Scripture: Luke 10:30–37

Summary: Jesus tells a story about a kind Samaritan.

Who is our Neighbour? **People Near Us, Fellow Human Beings**. Jesus expanded the concept of "neighbour" to include everyone we encounter, emphasising that we should treat all people with love and compassion, not just those who are geographically close to us. We need to share the word of God with them, that way we win them to Christ.

Lesson: We should help others, no matter who they are.

Prayer: Lord, help us to be kind and helpful to everyone. Amen.

Activity: Role-play the story of the Good Samaritan.

Now let us look at the skills needed to be good disciples of Jesus.

Day 13: Faith
Scripture: Hebrews 11: 1-6; Revelation 2:10

Faith is having strong belief and trust in Jesus. We need faith to be good disciples of Jesus, and for us to preach and perform miracles. Jesus even said we shall do greater works than He did. To exercise faith in God we must believe that He is, remain steadfast and loyal to God's calling.

Lesson: I have to trust and believe in God at all times.

Prayer: Oh Lord, help me to always have faith in you.

Action: List the situations where you need to exercise faith in God.

Day 14: Obedience
Scripture: John 14:15

Following Jesus' teachings and commandments.

Why do I need obedience to follow Jesus? Without obedience, no one can follow Jesus.

1. Guidance and Direction: Obeying Jesus' teachings provides a clear path for living a life that is pleasing to God. It helps disciples to know what is right and wrong and how to act in accordance with God's will.

2. Demonstrating Love for God
- **Expression of Love**: 1 John 5:3
- **Spiritual Growth:** When we love Jesus and obey Him, we will grow spiritually.

Prayer: Father, help me to obey you. When I do, that means I love you.

Day 15: Humility
Scripture: Philippians 2:3–4

Humility means being humble and putting others before oneself.

Humility is about recognising and accepting your limitations, being open to others' ideas and contributions, and having a realistic view of your strengths and weaknesses. Humility isn't about thinking less of yourself; it's about thinking of yourself less. Jesus Himself exemplified humility throughout His life and ministry by being humble.

Lesson: Without humility, we cannot be disciples of Jesus.

Prayer: Oh Lord, help me to be humble so that I can receive the grace to be a good disciple.

Action: Write what humility means to you.

Day 16: Prayerfulness
Scripture: 1 Thessalonians 5:17; Philippians 4:6

Why does a disciple of Jesus need to pray? Prayer is an essential practice for a disciple of Jesus, serving multiple purposes and offering profound benefits. Here are some reasons why prayer is crucial:

It's communication with God to build a relationship.

It allows us as disciples to share our thoughts, feelings, and desires with Him.

To seek guidance and wisdom.

To express dependence on God.

Lesson: Prayer is a vital aspect of discipleship.

Prayer: Father Lord, please help me to pray at all times.

Action: Draw the prayer hand and use it to pray daily.

Day 17: Servant Leadership
Scripture: Mark 10:45

Leading by serving others, and following Jesus' example. He exemplified servant leadership.

A servant leader is someone who prioritises the well-being and development of their team or followers above his/her own ambitions. This leadership style is characterised by a commitment to serving others, promoting growth, and building a supportive and empowering environment.

Qualities of a Servant Leader:

1. **Empathy**
2. **Listening**: Actively listening to the needs and concerns of others.
3. **Stewardship**: Managing resources responsibly and ethically.

Prayer: Jesus, help me to be a servant leader.

Action: List steps you can take to serve others today as a child.

Day 18: Forgiveness
Scripture: Colossians 3:13

Being willing to forgive others as Jesus forgives us.

What is Forgiveness?

Forgiveness is a profound and essential aspect of human relationships and personal growth. It involves letting go of resentment, anger, and the desire for revenge against someone who has wronged you. Instead, you choose to offer understanding, compassion, and peace.

Lesson: If I do not forgive others, God will not forgive me.

Prayer: Father, help me to forgive all those who have hurt me.

Action: Write the meaning of forgiveness, discuss forgiveness with a friend or family member.

Day 19: Generosity
Scripture: 2 Corinthians 9:7

Sharing resources and being generous towards others.

God has given us an example of giving by His one and only begotten son Jesus, we need to give back to God as His disciples. We need to be generous and cheerful as we give. We can give Him our lives, our time, our talents, skills, our money, etc.

Lesson: I cannot out-give God; He owns silver and gold.

Pray: Father, please help me to always give cheerfully to you.

Action: Make a list of the things you can give to God and how you will implement them.

Day 20: Patience
Scripture: James 1:2–4

Exercising patience and endurance through trials.
What is Patience?
Patience is the ability to wait, endure, or persevere through difficult situations without becoming angry, upset, or frustrated. It's a valuable quality that allows individuals to stay calm and composed while facing challenges, delays, or adversity. It can include, self-control, endurance, calmness, tolerance, etc.

Prayer: Oh Lord, help me to be patient to wait for your promises in my life.
Action: Write down what you would do when confronted with a situation that needs patience, example when you are requesting gift from parents.

Day 21: Witnessing
Scripture: Acts 1:8

Sharing the message of Jesus with others. Witnessing, as a disciple of Jesus, involves sharing the message of the gospel and one's personal faith journey with others. As a child, you can tell your friends in school about Jesus, how you love Him and all the things He has done for you. Through sharing your testimonies, your friends and acquaintances can come to know Jesus.

Lesson: Witnessing for Jesus is mandatory as a disciple of Jesus.

Prayer: Father, I pray that you give me the grace to witness for you.

Action: Tell someone about Jesus today.

Day 22: Knowledge of Scripture
Scripture: 2 Timothy 3:16–17

Understanding and applying the Bible in daily life.

As a human being, you cannot give what you do not have. As a child, you need to equip yourself with the knowledge of the word of God. When you know the word, you can use it to preach to people and then defend yourself when the devil wants to tempt you.

Lesson: You need to study the word of God to know it for yourself.

Prayer: Lord, help me to understand your word.

Action/Song:
Read your Bible
*Pray every day*3

In the next few days, we are going to study about the challenges a child can face as a disciple of Jesus and how to combat/overcome them.

Here are some common challenges and how to combat them:

Day 23: Overcoming Temptation
Scripture: 1 Corinthians 10:13

Challenge: If not handled well, temptations can lead disciples away from their faith and principles.

How to Combat: Stay vigilant and be prayerful, avoid situations that lead to temptation, and rely on the Holy Spirit for strength.

Lesson: God will not allow any temptation that is above us to come to us, His grace is sufficient.

Prayer: Oh Lord, please give me the grace, patience, wisdom, and skills that I need to overcome any temptation that comes my way.

Action: Write 2 temptations that have come your way recently and how you overcame them.

Day 24: Persecution
Scripture: Matthew 5:10

What is Persecution?

Persecution refers to the hostility and ill-treatment that people may face because of their beliefs, faith, or identity. For disciples of Jesus, persecution can manifest in various forms, ranging from social ostracism and discrimination to physical violence and imprisonment. We see that Paul and Silas were in prison for their faith in God, but God delivered them.

How to Combat Persecution:
- Strengthen your faith through prayer, studying the Bible, and finding support within a community of believers.
- Make Good friends to support you in difficult times.

Action: Discuss what you did when you faced persecution.

Day 25: Balancing Faith and Daily Life
Scripture: Colossians 3:17

In this generation, a lot of things like peer pressure, social media, quest for relevance, finance, etc, can pose a challenge to our daily Christian living if we are not careful. As a disciple of Christ, we may encounter doubts about our faith or God's plans.

How to Combat:

- Make time for prayer, Bible study, and fellowship regularly.
- Seek to see your daily activities as acts of worship.

Lesson: Challenges will come, Jesus has promised to be with me till the end.

Prayer: Lord, I pray that you help me overcome challenges in my daily life.

Day 26: Staying Spiritually Nourished
Scripture: John 15:4

"Remain in me, as I also remain in you. No branch can bear fruit by itself; it must remain in the vine. Neither can you bear fruit unless you remain in me."

Spiritual dryness or feeling distant from God. We need to stay connected to Jesus the vine so that we can draw strength from Him.

How to Combat:

- Regularly engage in spiritual exercises like prayer, fasting, studying scripture, and worship.
- Connect with a community that encourages spiritual growth, e.g. church.
- Listen to gospel music and messages.

Prayer: Lord, help me to stay connected to you.

Day 27: Sharing Faith Boldly
Scripture: Acts 4:29

As young people, you can have the fear of missing out (FOMO) or fear of rejection or inadequacy when sharing the gospel.

As a believer, you should not be discouraged because people also mocked Jesus.

How to Combat:

- Pray for courage, practice sharing your testimony, and trust in the Holy Spirit to guide your words and actions.

Lesson: The world will not always love me, because they did not love Jesus.

Prayer: Father, help me to always come to you as my best friend.

Action: Write about a time when you felt left out. What did you do?

Day 28: Dealing with Doubts and Uncertainty
Uncertainty
Scripture: Proverbs 3:5–6

As a growing child, there will be times when you have doubts about the gospel, do not let your heart be troubled, this is why Jesus said we should come to Him when we are heavy-laden.

How to Combat:

- Address doubt by seeking answers through prayer, scripture, and guidance from trusted mentors or spiritual leaders.
- Read Christian books on following Jesus.
- Listen to Christian songs.
- Listen and watch messages on discipleship.

Activity/Song: *My Hope is built on nothing less than Jesus Blood and Righteousness*

Day 29: Maintaining Humility
Scripture: Philippians 2:3

What is Humility?

Humility is the quality of having a modest view of one's own importance. It involves recognising one's limitations, being open to others' ideas, and valuing others equally or above oneself.

Pride is the antonym of humility. It can hinder spiritual growth and relationships with others. Sometimes, it can be hard to be humble as a disciple especially when God answers your prayers or uses you to do one miracle or the other. Be humble, God gives grace to the humble and resists the proud.

How to Combat:

- Practice humility by serving others, acknowledging your limitations, and continuously seeking God's guidance.

Day 30

What are some ways you can follow Jesus more closely?

List them

1. _______________________________________

2. _______________________________________

3. _______________________________________

4. _______________________________________

5. _______________________________________

6. _______________________________________

7. _______________________________________

Day 31: Complete the puzzle below

Word Search for Jesus' First Disciples

Find the words on the list that are hidden in the puzzle. The words can be left to right, up and down, or diagonally.

```
G A L I L E E F P C I N
A L I Q U A T U E R I A
L R S E C T E M T I T T
A A F O L L O W E D I H
M E Q U I M C I R L A A
B E L E P E E I R I U N
R E M O H O R S I T E A
D I S C I P L E S T V E
I A I B L E N I S I O L
N S M D I U G I A M A E
Q U O T P O N S E C T H
D O N O R A N D R E W U
```

ANDREW	FOLLOWED	LAMB	NATHANAEL	PHILIP
DISCIPLES	GALILEE	MESSIAH	PETER	SIMON

Word Search for
Jesus' First Disciples

Find the words on the list that are hidden in the puzzle. The words can be left to right, up and down, or diagonally.

ANDREW	FOLLOWED	LAMB	NATHANAEL	PHILIP
DISCIPLES	GALILEE	MESSIAH	PETER	SIMON

Notes

Easter, Jesus Died to Redeem Us and Make Us His Friends

APRIL

Introduction

Did you know that Easter is more than just a day for the Easter Bunny and egg hunts? The world has reduced Easter to a festive occasion, overlooking the important teachings and purpose behind it. This month, we will take children through the events leading up to Easter, the significance of Jesus' death and resurrection, and how they can apply these lessons in their lives. Please, on Good Friday and Easter Sunday, you can always go back to read and reference the story of the death and resurrection of Jesus.

Day 1: Jesus Enters Jerusalem
Scripture: Matthew 21:9

Summary: The air crackled with anticipation as Jesus entered Jerusalem. The crowds, a sea of faces, surged forward, their voices rising in a crescendo of praise. Children and adults with hope. "Hosanna!" they shouted, "Blessed is he who comes in the name of the Lord!" their voices echoed through the streets.

Lesson: Jesus is our redemption King who comes in peace.

Reflection: How can you welcome Jesus into your life?

Prayer: Dear Jesus, thank You for coming to us with love and peace.

Action: Make a palm branch craft and wave it as you say, "Hosanna!"

Day 2: Jesus Clears the Temple
Scripture: Matthew 21:12–13

Summary: Jesus went into the temple (church in our day). He saw people selling. Jesus was angry because the temple was for worship, not business. He turned over the tables of the money changers and sent them away. He wanted a place where people could pray to God without distractions.

Lesson: Jesus wants His house to be a place of prayer and worship.

Reflection: How can you show respect in places of worship?

Action/Prayer: Pray, asking God to help you keep your body holy as His Temple.

Day 3: The Last Supper
Scripture: Luke 22:19–20

Summary: Jesus and His friends were gathered together for a special meal. He said, "This bread is my body, given to you. Do this to remember me." Then, Jesus took a cup of wine, gave thanks, and shared it with his friends. He said, "This cup is the new covenant in my blood, poured out for you." With these words, Jesus was teaching His friends about a special promise and a sacrifice that would soon take place.

Lesson: Remember Jesus' sacrifice every time we take communion.
Reflection: How can you remember Jesus' love and sacrifice?
Prayer: Thank You, Jesus, for giving Your life for us.

Day 4: Jesus Washes the Disciples' Feet
Scripture: John 13:14–15

Summary: Jesus washes His disciples' feet as an act of service.

Jesus and His friends were having a special dinner. After the meal, Jesus did something surprising. He got up and started washing their feet! This was a job usually done by servants. Jesus wanted to teach His friends a lesson. He showed them that even the greatest person can serve others.

Lesson: Jesus teaches us to serve others humbly.

Reflection: How can you serve others like Jesus did?

Prayer: Lord, help us to serve others with love and humility.

Action: Do something kind for someone else.

Day 5: Jesus Prays in Gethsemane
Scripture: Matthew 26:39

Summary: Jesus prays in the garden, asking God for strength to face what is coming.

As powerful as Jesus is, He still prayed. He was going to bear the sin of the whole world on the cross, so He prayed to God to help Him.

Lesson: Jesus shows us the importance of prayer in difficult times.

Reflection: What do you need to pray about today?

Prayer: Jesus, thank You for showing us how to pray. Help us to seek God in our difficult times. Amen.

Action: Spend extra time praying alone today.

Day 6: Jesus is Betrayed
Scripture: Luke 22:48

Summary: Judas betrays Jesus with a kiss. Judas, one of Jesus' closest friends, had a secret plan. He was going to betray Jesus to the wicked men who wanted to hurt Him. This was a terrible thing to do, but Judas was greedy and selfish. It was a painful moment, a betrayal that would lead to Jesus' suffering and death.

Lesson: Betrayal hurts, but Jesus forgives.
Reflection: How can you forgive someone who has hurt you?
Prayer: Lord, help me to forgive others.
Action: Write a letter of forgiveness to someone who has hurt you.

Day 7: Peter Denies Jesus
Scripture: Luke 22:61–62

Summary: Peter denies knowing Jesus three times before the rooster crows.

Peter was very vocal and promised to be with Jesus, however, Jesus knew Peter was going to deny Him three times. This is because Peter did not have the power to withstand temptation. After receiving the Holy Spirit, he stood for Jesus.

Lesson: Jesus understands our weaknesses and forgives us.

Reflection: What do you understand by the word weakness? When have you needed forgiveness?

Prayer: Thank You, Jesus, for forgiving us even when we fail.

Action: Write down something you need to ask forgiveness for.

Day 8: Jesus Before Pilate
Scripture: Matthew 27:24

Summary: Pilate, the Roman leader, was in a difficult situation. He knew Jesus was innocent, but the angry crowd wanted Jesus punished. Pilate tried to reason with them, but they wouldn't listen. Pilate said, "You are the ones who want this." It was a sad day when a good man was wrongly condemned.

Lesson: Sometimes, people make wrong choices to please others.

Reflection: How can you stand up for what is right?

Prayer: Lord, help me to always choose what is right, even when it's hard.

Action: Talk about a time you stood up for what was right.

Day 9: Jesus is Mocked
Scripture: Matthew 27:29–30

Summary: The soldiers mocked Jesus, placing a crown of thorns on His head.
When He was thirsty, He asked for water and they gave Him sour vinegar. They laughed at Him and said, "If you are the King of Jews, save yourself." It was indeed a horrible experience.

Lesson: Jesus endured suffering and humiliation for our sake.
Reflection: How can you show gratitude for Jesus' sacrifice?
Prayer: Jesus, thank You for enduring so much for us. Help us to live for You. Amen.
Action: Make a crown of thorns craft and discuss its significance.

Day 10: Jesus is Crucified
Scripture: Luke 23:33

Summary: Jesus is nailed to the cross.

This is a very remarkable and significant event in Christianity. When the blood of Jesus dropped on the earth, there was an earthquake and complete darkness. The curtain dividing the holy place and the Holy of Holies was torn apart. This signifies that we now have access to God at anytime and anywhere unlike in the Old Testament.

Lesson: Jesus' death shows His great love for us.

Reflection: How can you show love to others like Jesus did?

Action: Draw a cross and write "Jesus loves me" on it.

Day 11: The Thief on the Cross
Scripture: Luke 23:42–43

Summary: When Jesus was on the cross, there were two criminals hanging beside Him. One of the criminals made fun of Jesus, but the other criminal knew that Jesus was innocent. He said to Jesus, "Please remember me when you come into your kingdom." Jesus promised the kind criminal, "Today you will be with me in paradise."

Lesson: Jesus forgives and promises eternal life to those who believe in Him.

Reflection: Why did Jesus promise the kind criminal on the cross that he will be in His paradise?

Prayer: Thank You, Jesus, for Your promise of eternal life.

Day 12: Jesus Dies
Scripture: John 19:30

Summary: Jesus says, "It is finished," and dies.

Jesus was suffering on the cross. He was tired and hurt. He said, "It is finished." With these words, Jesus showed that He had completed the work that God had sent Him for. He had sacrificed His life to save people from their sins. After saying these words, Jesus died.

Lesson: Jesus completed the work of salvation on the cross.

Reflection: How does Jesus' sacrifice impact your life?

Prayer: Thank You, Jesus, for finishing the work of salvation for us.

Action: Spend some quiet time reflecting on Jesus' sacrifice.

Day 13: Jesus is Buried
Scripture: Matthew 27:59–60

Summary: Jesus is laid in a tomb.
As prophesied in the Old Testament, His body was taken by Joseph of Arimathea, a rich man, and buried.

Lesson: Jesus' burial shows that He truly died for our sins.
Reflection: How does it make you feel to know Jesus died for you?
Prayer: Lord, thank You for dying and being buried for our sins. Amen.
Action: Draw a picture of Jesus' tomb.

Song: *I need no other argument,*
I need no other plea…,
It is enough that Jesus died,
and that he died for me

Day 14: The Tomb is Sealed
Scripture: Matthew 27:65–66

Summary: Guards are placed at the tomb to ensure it stays sealed.

After Jesus was buried, the religious leaders, concerned about the prophecy of His resurrection, asked Pontius Pilate to secure the tomb. As a result, the tomb was sealed and guarded by Roman soldiers to prevent anyone from taking the body.

Lesson: God's plans cannot be stopped.

Reflection: How can you trust in God's plans even when things seem impossible?

Prayer: God, help us to trust Your plans no matter what.

Action: Discuss a time when something seemed impossible but turned out okay.

Day 15: The Women Visit the Tomb
Scripture: Matthew 28:1

Summary: Mary Magdalene and the other Mary go to see the tomb of Jesus at dawn to honour His body. They were filled with sorrow and grief. They loved Jesus and sought to see Him.

Lesson: Seek Jesus even when it's difficult.

Reflection: How can you seek Jesus in your everyday life?

- By praying and talking to God.
- By reading His word, the Bible.
- By teaching others the word of God.

Prayer: Jesus, help us to seek You every day, even when it's hard. Amen.

Action: Spend time reading a Bible story.

Day 16: The Resurrection
Scripture: Matthew 28:5–6

Summary: On the third day, Mary Magdalene and the other Mary went to Jesus' tomb. They saw that the stone covering the tomb had been rolled away. Suddenly, an angel appeared to them. His appearance was bright as lightning, and his clothes were white as snow. The women were terrified, but the angel spoke to them, calming their fears.

Lesson: Jesus is alive!

Reflection: How does Jesus' resurrection give you hope?

Prayer: Thank You, Jesus, for rising from the dead and giving us hope. Amen.

Action: Make a "He is Risen" banner to celebrate.

Song: *He arose …he arose…Hallelujah, Christ arose.*

Day 17: Jesus Appears to Mary Magdalene
Magdalene
Scripture: John 20:16

Summary: After Jesus' crucifixion and burial, Mary Magdalene went to the tomb early on the first day of the week and found that the stone had been rolled away from the entrance. Distressed, she ran to tell Peter and John, who then came to see the empty tomb. After Peter and John left, Mary stayed outside the tomb, weeping. As she wept, she bent and saw angels who told her, "Jesus is risen, He is no more in the grave."

Lesson: Jesus comforts us in our sorrow.
Reflection: When have you felt Jesus' comfort?
Prayer: Thank You, Jesus, for comforting me when I am sad.

Day 18: Jesus Appears to the Disciples
Scripture: Luke 24:36

Summary: Jesus appears to His disciples and says, "Peace be with you."

Jesus' friends were in a house, and they locked the doors because they were scared. They didn't know what was going to happen next.

Jesus Came to Visit:

- Even though the doors were locked, Jesus suddenly stood among them.

The Disciples Were Happy:

- When they saw Jesus, they were so happy and excited!

Lesson: Jesus brings peace to our hearts.

Prayer: Lord, thank You for bringing us peace and tranquility.

Action: Tell a story of when you felt peace in your heart.

All these proofs of death on the cross, resurrection, and appearing to Mary, His disciples and many others are what differentiates Christianity from other religions.

JESUS DIED ON THE CROSS TO MAKE US HIS FRIENDS, HOW CAN WE BE GOOD FRIENDS?

Day 19: Jesus, Our Best Friend
Scripture: John 15:13

Summary: Imagine a world where people don't like you just because you are a follower of Jesus. They might make fun of you, call you names, or even hurt you. Jesus knew this would happen to His friends, so He told them. We can trust that God is always with us, protecting and guiding us.

Lesson: Jesus showed the greatest love by laying down His life for us.

Reflection: How does it feel to know that Jesus calls you His friend?

Prayer: Dear Jesus, thank You for being our best friend.

Song: *What a friend we have in Jesus*

Day 20: The Importance of Friendship
Scripture: Ecclesiastes 4:9–10

Summary: Two heads are better than one. It's always nice to have someone to talk to. When you work with someone, you can encourage each other and share ideas. It's like having a partner who can help you carry your burdens. And when you're feeling down, your friend can cheer you up and give you hope.

Lesson: Friends help each other and lift each other up.

Reflection: How can you be a better friend to those around you?

Prayer: Lord, help us to be supportive and encouraging friends.

Action: Do something kind for a friend today.

Day 21: Choosing Good Friends
Scripture: Proverbs 13:20

Summary: Once upon a time, there was a young boy named Alfred. Alfred was a curious and bright boy, always eager to learn. He likes listening to wise stories and seeking knowledge from the elders of his village. He loved to spend time with the wise old man, Edward, who was known for his wisdom and understanding.

Lesson: Choosing wise friends helps us grow.

Reflection: Are your friends helping you grow closer to God?

Prayer: God, help us to choose friends who lead us closer to You. Amen.

Action: Tell a story of the last time you spent time with a friend who encouraged your faith.

Day 22: Being a Loyal Friend
Scripture: Proverbs 17:17

Summary: A true friend is always there, like a gift from God. They stick by you, no matter what. They're like a cool drink on a hot day or a warm blanket on a cold night. So, be grateful for your true friends and cherish them always.

Lesson: A true friend loves at all times and is always there.

Reflection: How can you show loyalty to your friends?

Prayer: Dear God, help us to be loyal and loving friends.

Action: Reach out to a friend you haven't spoken to in a while.

Day 23: Forgiving Friends
Scripture: Colossians 3:13

Summary: Imagine a world filled with kindness and forgiveness. A place where people are patient with each other and are always ready to help. This is the kind of world that God wants us to live in. Forgive as the Lord forgave. When we forgive others, we are showing love and compassion, just like Jesus did.

Lesson: Forgive others just as the Lord has forgiven you.

Reflection: Is there a friend you need to forgive?

Prayer: Lord, help us to forgive our friends as You have forgiven us. Amen.

Action: Forgive a friend who has hurt you.

Day 24: Encouraging Friends
Scripture: 1 Thessalonians 5:11

Summary: Imagine you're building a house. You wouldn't just throw bricks together, right? You'd carefully place each one, making sure it fits perfectly with the others. That's kind of how we should treat each other. We should build one another up, encouraging and supporting one another. We can lift each other up, help each other through tough times, and celebrate each other's successes.

Lesson: Encourage one another and build them up.

Reflection: How can you encourage your friends today?

Prayer: Jesus, help us to be encouragers to our friends.

Action: Write an encouraging note to a friend.

Day 25: Friends Share Joy and Sorrow
Scripture: Romans 12:15

Summary: Imagine you're playing a game with your friends.

You wouldn't want to just play for yourself, right? You'd want everyone to have fun and feel included. We should try to make others happy and feel better. And when they're sad, we should be there to comfort them. By doing this, we show love and compassion, just like Jesus did.

Lesson: Rejoice with those who rejoice; mourn with those who mourn.

Prayer: God, help us to share in the joys and sorrows of our friends. Amen.

Action: Celebrate a friend's joy or offer comfort in their sorrow.

Day 26: Friends Pray for Each Other
Scripture: James 5:16

Summary: A friend is someone who offers companionship, support and kindness. We should support, trust and pray for our friends. Think of their well-being and be there for them when there is a problem or sorrow. It provides emotional support, joy, and a sense of belonging. Cherishing and nurturing your friendships can lead to lifelong, meaningful connections.

Lesson: Pray for one another so that you may be healed.

Reflection: How can you pray for your friends today?

Prayer: Dear Jesus, help us to pray for our friends every day.

Action: Pray for your friends by name today.

Day 27: Serving Friends
Scripture: Galatians 5:13

Summary: Imagine you're a bird flying high in the sky. You're free to go wherever you want, right? But just because you're free doesn't mean you can do whatever you want. You still need to be kind and helpful to others. So, even though we're free to do what we want, we should choose to love and help others. That's what it means to be truly free.

Reflection: How can you serve your friends with love?

Prayer: Lord, help us to serve our friends with humility and love.

Action: Do a kind act of service for a friend.

Day 28: Friends Share Truth
Scripture: Ephesians 4:15

Summary: We're all like puzzle pieces, each one unique and special. When we fit together, we create a beautiful picture. This means that we should be honest and kind to each other. When we work together and love each other, we can grow stronger and become more like Jesus.

Lesson: Speak the truth in love.
Reflection: How can you share the truth with your friends in love?
Prayer: Jesus, help us to speak the truth in love to our friends. Amen.
Action: Have an honest and loving conversation with a friend.

Day 29: Reflection
Scripture: Luke 19:10

Summary: Jesus came to earth to bring hope to the hopeless, healing to the broken, and salvation to the lost. As a good friend, He does not discriminate and is compassionate. This is how He wants us to behave.

- What is the message of Easter and what do we celebrate in Easter?
- What happened to Jesus after He died?
- What kind of friend do you think you are?
- What kind of friend was Jesus?
- Make a list of some of your friends and what kind of friends they are.

Day 30

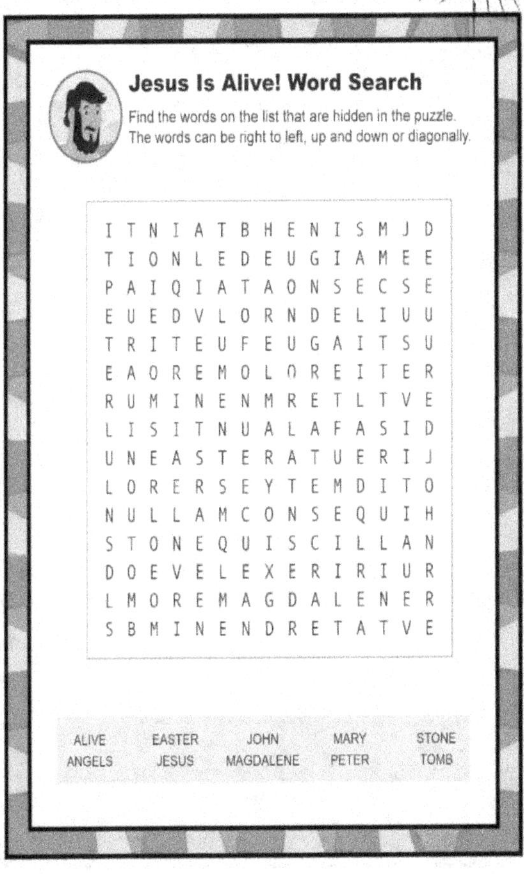

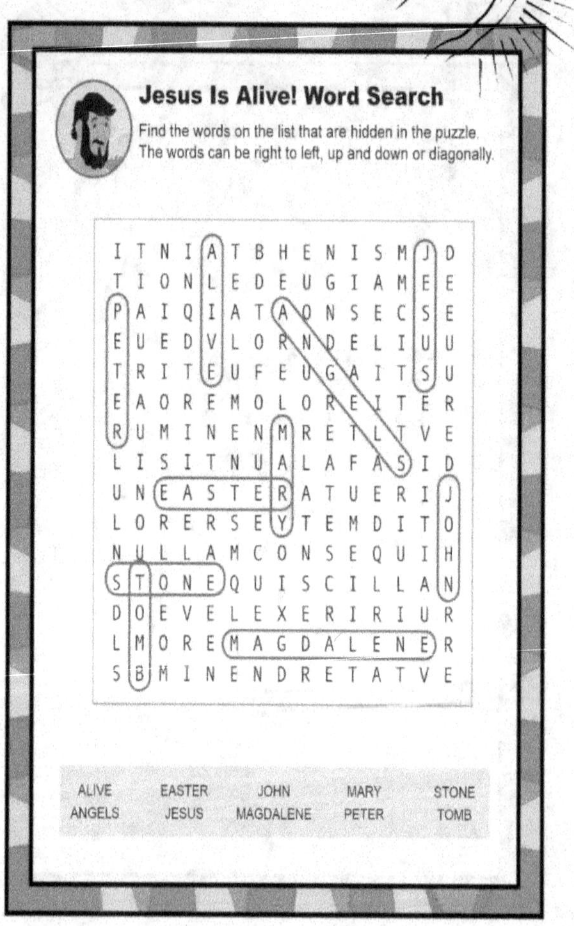
Jesus Is Alive! Word Search
Find the words on the list that are hidden in the puzzle.
The words can be right to left, up and down or diagonally.
I T N I A T B H E N I S M J D
T I O N L E D E U G I A M E E
P A I Q I A T A O N S E C S E
E U E D V L O R N D E L I U U
T R I T E U F E U G A I T S U
E A O R E M O L O R E I T E R
R U M I N E N M R E T L T V E
L I S I T N U A L A F A S I D
U N E A S T E R A T U E R I J
L O R E R S E Y T E M D I T O
N U L L A M C O N S E Q U I H
S T O N E Q U I S C I L L A N
D O E V E L E X E R I R I U R
L M O R E M A G D A L E N E R
S B M I N E N D R E T A T V E
ALIVE   EASTER   JOHN   MARY   STONE
ANGELS   JESUS   MAGDALENE   PETER   TOMB

Notes

MAY

May

The Holy Spirit

Introduction

This month, we will be studying about the Holy Spirit. The Holy Spirit is a central figure in Christianity, representing God's presence and power in the world and in the lives of believers. The Holy Spirit is the third person of the Holy Trinity, alongside God the Father and God the Son (Jesus Christ).

The Holy Spirit is the Presence of God

The Holy Spirit is seen as God's presence within believers, guiding, comforting, and empowering us to live according to His will.

The Giver of Life

The Holy Spirit is often described as the breath or life-giving force of God.

Day 1: Who is the Holy Spirit?

Summary: Jesus promises the Holy Spirit will be our helper.

The Holy Spirit is a person, and Has feelings. He can become sad when others insult and blaspheme against Him (Is 63:10; Matt 12:31; Ac 7:51; Eph 4:30; Heb 10:29).

He has intentions. He communicates, testifies, teaches, and comforts. These are qualities that distinguish Him as a person.

Lesson: The Holy Spirit is our guide and comforter.

Prayer: Holy Spirit, thank You for being with us and helping us. Amen.

Activity: Draw a picture of a dove, symbolising the Holy Spirit.

Day 2: The Holy Spirit at Pentecost
Scripture: Acts 2:1–4

Summary: On the day of Pentecost, suddenly, a mighty wind filled the room, and flames descended on them. The Holy Spirit came upon the believers. They spoke in different languages, and people from many nations heard the good news of Jesus. Peter explained that this was what the prophet Joel had foretold. Many people believed and were baptised.

Lesson: The Holy Spirit gives us power to be witnesses for Jesus.
Prayer: Holy Spirit, fill us with Your power. Amen.
Activity: Make paper flames and discuss the story of Pentecost.

Day 3: The Fruit of the Spirit
There are 9 *fruit* of the Holy Spirit.
Scripture: Galatians 5:22–23

Summary: Imagine a garden with beautiful fruits. The Holy Spirit is like a gardener who helps us grow these *fruit*. The *fruit* of the Spirit includes love, joy, peace, patience, kindness, goodness, faithfulness, gentleness and self-control. When people observe these *fruit* in our life, they speak good of us and glorify God in heaven.

Lesson: The Holy Spirit helps us show these qualities in our lives.
Prayer: Holy Spirit, grow Your *fruit* in our hearts. Amen.
Activity: Draw a tree with the nine *fruit* of the Spirit.

Day 4: Love
Scripture: 1 Corinthians 13:4–7

Summary: Love is patient and kind. Love is patient, like waiting for your turn to play with your favourite toy. Love is kind, like sharing your snack. Love doesn't envy, or brag, it is not rude or selfish. It doesn't get angry easily and doesn't keep track of wrongs. It never gives up. Love is like a warm blanket on a cold night, comforting and safe, bringing hope.

Lesson: Let's show love in all we do, just like God loves us.

Prayer: Holy Spirit, help us to love others. Amen.

Activity: Make and decorate love hearts to give to your family.

Day 5: Joy
Scripture: Philippians 4:4

Summary: Rejoice in the Lord always. Always be happy.

Have you ever felt sad or worried? Everyone does sometimes. The Bible tells us to always be happy and joyful. We can be happy because God loves us very much, is always with us, even when we feel lonely or scared. We can find joy in simple things, trusting that God will always take care of us.

Lesson: The Holy Spirit fills us with joy.
Prayer: Holy Spirit, fill our hearts with joy. Amen.
Activity: Draw or write things that make you joyful.

Day 6: Peace
Scripture: John 14:27

Summary: Jesus gives us His peace.
Jesus told His friends, "Peace I leave with you; my peace I give to you. I do not give to you as the world gives. Do not let your hearts be troubled and do not be afraid."
Imagine a warm, cozy blanket on a cold night. That's how God's peace feels. It's a calm feeling inside. Even when things are scary or confusing, ask God for His peace.

Lesson: The Holy Spirit brings peace into our lives.
Prayer: Holy Spirit, fill us with Your peace. Amen.
Activity: Make a peace dove craft.

Day 7: Patience
Scripture: Ephesians 4:2

Summary: Be patient and kind, bearing with one another in love.

Have you ever waited for something you really wanted? Maybe a new toy or a special treat? Waiting can be hard, but it can also teach us important lessons. The Bible tells us to be "gentle and patient." Being patient means waiting calmly and quietly. It means not getting frustrated when things don't happen right away. Let's practice being patient.

Lesson: When we're patient, we show others that we care.

Prayer: Holy Spirit, give us patience in all situations. Amen.

Activity: Play a game that requires patience.

Day 8: Kindness
Scripture: Ephesians 4:32

Summary: There was a girl named Lily. Lily loved to play with her friends, but sometimes they would argue and Lily would feel angry. One day, Lily's mom read her a Bible story. Jesus taught His followers to be kind and forgiving, just like God forgives us. Lily wanted to be like Jesus.

The next time Lily and her friends argued, she apologised and asked for forgiveness.

Lesson: The Holy Spirit helps us to be kind to others.

Prayer: Holy Spirit, help us to show kindness every day. Amen.

Activity: Make kindness cards to give to others.

Day 9: Goodness
Scripture: Psalm 23:6

Summary: David was a shepherd boy who loved his sheep. He felt safe and was loved by God. One day, a big storm came. David was scared, but he remembered Jesus' promise: "I will always be with you." With courage, David faced the storm, trusting in Jesus, the Good Shepherd. When the storm ended, the sun shone, reminding David of God's love and protection.

Lesson: The Holy Spirit helps us to do good.

Prayer: Holy Spirit, help us to do good and follow Your ways. Amen.

Activity: Plan a good deed and carry it out.

Day 10: Faithfulness
Scripture: Lamentations 3:22–23

Summary: Esther hurt her knee and felt sad. Her grandma read her a Bible verse about God's faithfulness. It said, *"The Lord's loving kindnesses indeed never cease, For His compassions never fail"*. Esther realised God was faithful, even when she was hurt. She felt better, knowing God would keep His promise to heal her. "They are new every morning; great is Your faithfulness." Esther felt comforted by these words.

Lesson: The Holy Spirit helps us to be faithful.

Prayer: Holy Spirit, help us to be faithful in all we do.

Activity: Create a faithfulness pledge card.

Day 11: Gentleness
Scripture: Philippians 4:5

Summary: Let your gentleness be evident to all.

There was a little boy named Samuel. Samuel was a very energetic boy who loved to play, but sometimes he could be a bit rough with his friends. His friends didn't enjoy playing with him and told him to be gentle. Samuel didn't quite understand what it meant to be gentle. So, his mom explained that being gentle meant being empathic, cautious, and considerate of others.

Lesson: Always be gentle with others.
Prayer: Holy Spirit, help us to be gentle and kind. Amen.
Activity: Role-play scenarios showing gentleness.

Day 12: Self-Control
Scripture: 2 Timothy 1:7

Summary: God gave us a spirit of self-discipline.

Lily was a very impatient girl who wanted everything right away. One day, Lily's grandma read her a verse from the Bible: "For God did not give us a spirit of timidity, but a spirit of power, of love, and of self-control." She realised that she could choose to be calm and patient.

Lesson: The Holy Spirit helps us to have self-control.

Prayer: Holy Spirit, help us to control our actions and words. Amen.

Activity: Make a list of situations where you can practice self-control.

Gifts of the Holy Spirit (1 Cor 12:8–10)

Now that we know who the Holy Spirit is and the *fruit* of the Holy Spirit, let us look at the gifts. Gifts of Wisdom, Knowledge, Faith, Healing, Miraculous Powers, Prophecy, Discernment of spirits, Speaking of different tongues, and Interpretation of tongues are gifts of the Holy Spirit.

It's important to remember that the *fruit* of the Holy Spirit, such as love, joy, peace, patience, kindness, goodness, faithfulness, gentleness, and self-control are different from the gifts of the Holy Spirit. The *fruit* (all nine combined is referred to as "fruit" not "fruits" because God wants us to have all of them) is a result of the Holy Spirit living within us, shaping our character, while the gifts are specific abilities given to us to help us serve God and others. For instance, the gift of Faith helps trust God and perform miracles.

Day 13: The Gift of Wisdom
Scripture: James 1:5

Summary: If anyone lacks wisdom, let them ask God.

The Bible tells us that if we need wisdom, we can ask God for it. He gives generously to everyone who asks. "Can I really ask God for wisdom?" one may ask. "Absolutely yes!" God gives us wisdom to make good choices when we ask through prayer.

Lesson: The Holy Spirit gives us wisdom to make good choices.

Prayer: Holy Spirit, give us wisdom in everything we do. Amen.

Activity: Write down a wise decision you made recently.

Day 14: The Gift of Knowledge
Scripture: 1 Corinthians 12:8

Summary: Ben was a curious boy. He loved to learn new things, but sometimes he felt overwhelmed by all the information. He wished he could understand everything easily. One day, Ben's teacher told the class about the Holy Spirit, who gives special gifts to believers. One of these gifts is knowledge. That night, Ben asked God for the gift of knowledge.

Lesson: The Holy Spirit helps us to understand God's truths.

Prayer: Holy Spirit, help us to know and understand Your Word. Amen.

Activity: Share something new you learnt about God.

Day 15: The Gift of Faith
Scripture: 1 Corinthians 12:9

Summary: Ever wondered, "Why do some people seem so brave when things are tough?" God gives us faith. Faith is like a strong rope that helps us climb over obstacles. Does it mean you are not scared if you have faith? Absolutely not! Faith is trusting in God, knowing that no matter what is happening, God has the best plans and will make things all right.

Lesson: The Holy Spirit strengthens our faith.

Prayer: Holy Spirit, help our faith to grow stronger. Amen.

Activity: Create a faith collage with words that inspire you.

Day 16: The Gift of Healing
Scripture: 1 Corinthians 12:9

Summary: God gives special gifts to people.
Have you been sick before? How did you feel? Nasty right? Healing is a gift. Some people can pray for the sick, and God will make them well. Jesus healed many people, and He still heals today through His followers. It's amazing how God uses people to show His love and power.

Lesson: The Holy Spirit can use us to bring healing to others.
Prayer: Holy Spirit, help us to pray for those who are sick. Amen.
Activity: Pray for someone who is sick.

Day 17: The Gift of Miracles
Scripture: 1 Corinthians 12:10

Summary: Noah couldn't speak. His parents prayed for a miracle that Noah could speak again, and God gave him the gift of speech. Noah used his gift to praise God and share the good news. God can do amazing things! All we have to do is to ask, believe and trust in Him.

Lesson: The Holy Spirit can do amazing things through us including healing others.
Prayer: Holy Spirit, help us to believe in Your power. Amen.
Activity: Tell a story of a Bible miracle that amazes you.

Day 18: The Gift of Prophecy
Scripture: 1 Corinthians 12:10

Summary: The Spirit gives the gift of prophecy.

Alfie was a quiet boy. One day, while praying, he began to speak words he didn't understand. Strange words, filled with meaning, flowed from his lips. Alfie's words were prophecies, inspired by the Holy Spirit. Alfie used this gift to comfort others and warn them of danger. He became a source of hope for his community.

Lesson: The Holy Spirit can give us messages from God.

Prayer: Holy Spirit, help us to hear and speak Your words. Amen.

Activity: Write a prayer asking for guidance.

Day 19: The Gift of Discernment
Scripture: 1 Corinthians 12:10

Summary: The Spirit gives the gift of discernment.

God gives special gifts to people. One of such gifts is discernment. This means being able to tell what is right and wrong. It helps us make good choices. With this gift, we can understand God's will and follow His guidance. We can also use this gift to know when to stay away from some people and events.

Lesson: The Holy Spirit helps us to know right from wrong.

Prayer: Holy Spirit, help us to make wise choices. Amen.

Activity: Discuss a situation where you need discernment.

Day 20: The Gift of Tongues
Scripture: 1 Corinthians 12:10

Summary: Joshua and David loved to pray together, often spending hours talking to God. One day, something extraordinary happened. Joshua began to speak in a language they didn't recognise. David was amazed but not afraid. He listened intently and began to understand the meaning behind the words. He interpreted the language, translating Joshua's words into their native tongue. The people around them were astounded.

Lesson: The Holy Spirit helps us to pray in new ways.

Prayer: Holy Spirit, help us to pray in tongues. Amen.

Activity: Learn a simple prayer in another language.

Day 21: The Gift of Interpretation
Scripture: 1 Corinthians 12:10

Summary: The Spirit gives the gift of interpreting tongues. God gives special gifts to people. One of such gifts is the gift of interpretation. Some people can understand the meaning of a message or vision. This helps others understand God's word better. It's amazing how God uses people to share His message with the world.

Lesson: The Holy Spirit helps us to understand messages from God.

Prayer: Holy Spirit, help us to understand and share Your messages. Amen.

Activity: Talk about a time you needed help understanding something.

Day 22: Fruit of the Spirit Review
Scripture: Galatians 5:22–23

Summary: Review all nine *fruit* of the Spirit. Imagine a beautiful garden with many fruits. The Holy Spirit helps us grow these *fruit* in our hearts. These *fruit* are love, joy, peace, patience, kindness, goodness, faithfulness, gentleness, and self-control. Let's grow these *fruit* and be like Jesus! We are like Jesus and then should have these *fruit* like Him.

Lesson: The Holy Spirit helps us show all these qualities.

Prayer: Holy Spirit, continue to grow Your *fruit* in us. Amen.

Activity: Create a fruit salad and talk about each *fruit* of the Spirit.

Day 23: Gifts of the Spirit Review
Scripture: 1 Corinthians 12:4–11

Summary: Review all nine gifts of the Spirit.

The Holy Spirit is like a special helper from God. He gives us gifts to help us. Some people can heal others, some can speak in different languages, and some can teach God's Word. These gifts help us to love and serve God and others.

Lesson: The Holy Spirit gives us gifts to help others.

Prayer: Holy Spirit, thank You for the gifts You give us. Amen.

Activity: Draw a gift box and write the gifts of the Spirit inside.

Day 24: The Holy Spirit Helps Us to Pray
Scripture: Romans 8:26

Summary: Sometimes we don't know how to pray especially when we are overwhelmed with events. Let's learn what the Bible says: *"Likewise the Spirit helps us in our weakness. For we do not know what to pray for as we ought, but the Spirit himself intercedes for us with groanings too deep for words"*.

Lesson: The Holy Spirit prays for us when we don't know what to pray.

Prayer: Holy Spirit, thank You for praying for us. Amen.

Activity: Write down a prayer and ask the Holy Spirit to help you pray.

Day 25: The Holy Spirit Comforts Us
Scripture: John 14:16

Summary: The Holy Spirit is our Comforter.

Samuel had lost his dog. A beautiful pet dog he had since he was born and felt so sad and alone. He prayed to the Holy Spirit for comfort. The Holy Spirit gave him peace and guidance, showing him that He was always with him.

Lesson: The Holy Spirit comforts us when we are sad or scared.

Prayer: Holy Spirit, thank You for Your comfort. Amen.

Activity: Make a comfort jar with notes of encouragement.

Day 26: The Holy Spirit Teaches Us
Scripture: John 14:26

Summary: Peter had spent the entire night fishing, but his nets were empty. Discouraged, he sat on the beach, he remembered his mother's words about the Holy Spirit, the teacher sent by God. He prayed, asking the Holy Spirit to guide him. Suddenly, Jesus invited him to go back out to the sea. Peter cast his net once more and the net was filled with so many fishes.

Lesson: The Holy Spirit can teach us many things.

Prayer: Holy Spirit, teach us Your truth. Amen.

Activity: Share something new you've learnt about God.

Day 27: Review
Scripture: Acts 13:2; Rom. 8:26–27

Who is the Holy Spirit?

The Holy Spirit is a person. The Holy Spirit is the third person of the Trinity, along with God the Father and God the Son. The Holy Spirit plays a vital role in the life of a believer, empowering him to live a godly life. He convicts the world of sin. He regenerates believers, giving them new life in Christ. He indwells in believers, enabling and empowering them to live a victorious life, overcoming sin and temptation. He has intentions, comforts, communicates, testifies, teaches, and prays.

Day 28: Revise the Fruit and Gifts of the Holy Spirit

The Holy Spirit, a divine gift from God, empowers believers with various spiritual gifts. These gifts, such as healing, prophecy, and speaking in tongues, are bestowed upon individuals to serve God's purposes.

Additionally, the Holy Spirit produces godly character traits known as the *fruit* of the Spirit. These include love, joy, peace, patience, kindness, goodness, faithfulness, gentleness, and self-control.

By cultivating these *fruit,* believers can live lives that reflect the love and grace of God.
What gifts do you think you have?
How can you develop them?

Day 29: Reflection

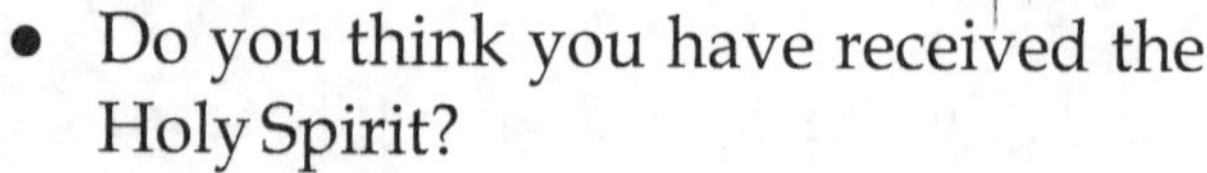

- Do you think you have received the Holy Spirit?
- Do you think the Holy Spirit is your helper?
- Make a list of how the Holy Spirit has helped your life.
- Write down what you wish the Holy Spirit to help you pray about.
- How can you maintain the *fruit* of the Holy Spirit?

Day 30

- What gifts of the Holy Spirit do you desire?
- Write them down.
- Take some time to pray for them.
- What *fruit* of the Holy Spirit do you think you lack?
- Write them down.
- Take some time to pray for them.

Day 31

Peter Preached with Boldness

Notes

June

The Parables of Jesus

Introduction

This month, we will be studying the different parables of Jesus.

Each day includes a scripture reference, a brief summary of the parable, a lesson, a prayer, and an activity.

Day 1: The Sower and the Seeds
Scripture: Matthew 13:1–9

Summary: A farmer went out to plant seeds. Some seeds fell on a path where birds ate them. Other seeds fell on rocks and the sun dried them. Some seeds fell among thorns that choked the plants. But some seeds fell on good soil and grew into beautiful plants. Jesus said that the good soil represents people who hear God's word and understand it.

Lesson: The condition of our hearts affects how we receive God's Word.
Prayer: Dear God, help us to have hearts ready to receive Your Word. Amen.
Activity: Discuss what plants need to grow.

Day 2: The Mustard Seed
Scripture: Matthew 13:31–32

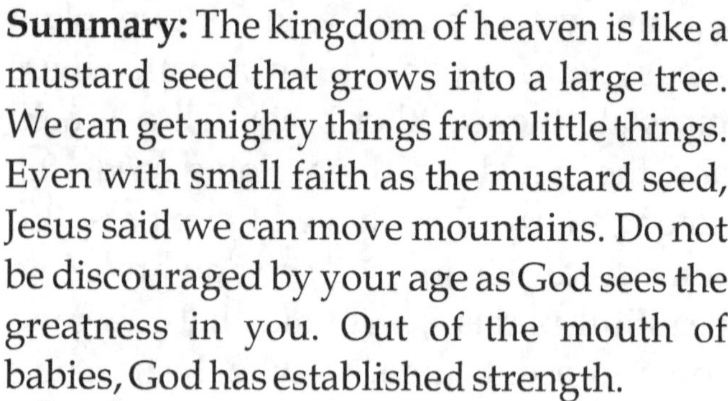

Summary: The kingdom of heaven is like a mustard seed that grows into a large tree. We can get mighty things from little things. Even with small faith as the mustard seed, Jesus said we can move mountains. Do not be discouraged by your age as God sees the greatness in you. Out of the mouth of babies, God has established strength.

Lesson: Small things can grow into great things with God.

Prayer: Lord, help our faith to grow strong like the mustard seed. Amen.

Activity: Draw a mustard seed and tree.

Day 3: The Yeast
Scripture: Matthew 13:33

Summary: The kingdom of heaven is like yeast that makes a dough rise.

Jesus told a story about the Kingdom of Heaven. He said it's like a tiny bit of yeast that a woman hides in a big pile of flour. Although small, the yeast works its way through the whole dough, making it rise. In the same way, the Kingdom of Heaven starts small but grows and spreads, changing lives and making the world a better place.

Lesson: God's kingdom grows quietly and steadily.

Prayer: Jesus, help us to see Your work in small, everyday things. Amen.

Activity: Bake bread together.

Day 4: The Hidden Treasure
Scripture: Matthew 13:44

Summary: A man finds treasure in a field and sells all he has to buy the field.
A farmer found a treasure hidden in a field. He was so excited! He sold everything he had to buy the field. The treasure was more valuable than anything else. It was like finding Jesus, the greatest treasure of all.

Lesson: God's kingdom is worth more than anything we have.
Prayer: Lord, help us to value Your kingdom above all else. Amen.
Activity: Hide small treasures and have a treasure hunt.

Day 5: The Pearl of Great Value
Scripture: Matthew 13:45–46

Summary: Once upon a time, there was a merchant who loved to search for beautiful pearls. One day, he found a pearl so special and precious that he sold everything he owned to buy it. This pearl was more valuable to him than anything else in the world. Jesus told this story to show us that God's kingdom is like that special pearl. It's so precious that we should give up anything to be a part of it.

Lesson: The kingdom of heaven is so precious and valuable.

Prayer: God, let us seek Your kingdom with all our hearts. Amen.

Activity: Make pearl necklaces with beads.

Day 6: The Net
Scripture: Matthew 13:47–50

Summary: Fishermen catch fish of all kinds in a net and then sorted them.

Once, Jesus told a story about a big net that was thrown into the sea. It caught all kinds of fish, good and bad. When the net was full, the fishermen pulled it to the shore. They sorted the good fish and put them in buckets. The bad fish they threw away. This story shows us that God will one day judge everyone.

Lesson: We as humans are like fishes to God here on earth as the fishes to the fishermen in the sea. There will be a final judgment day when the good is separated from the evil.

Prayer: Jesus, help us to live in a way that pleases You. Amen.

Activity: Draw different kinds of fish and sort them.

Day 7: The Lost Sheep
Scripture: Luke 15:3–7

Summary: A shepherd had a hundred sheep and lost one. The shepherd leaves the ninety-nine sheep to find the one that is lost. Jesus looks out for any of us, even if I am the only one on earth, Jesus would have still died for me. The Bible says that it is not the will of God that anyone should perish. God desires that everyone be saved.

Lesson: God cares for each of us individually.
Prayer: Thank You, Jesus, for seeking and saving the lost. Amen.
Activity: Play a game of hide and seek.

Day 8: The Lost Coin
Scripture: Luke 15:8–10

Summary: A woman searches for a lost coin and rejoices when she finds it. A woman had ten silver coins. She lost one! She searched high and low, lit a lamp, and swept the floor. When she found it, she was so happy! She called her friends and neighbours to celebrate. Just like the woman, God is happy when we come back to Him.

Lesson: God rejoices when a sinner repents.
Prayer: Lord, thank You for celebrating our return to You. Amen.
Activity: Have a coin hunt.

Day 9: The Prodigal Son
Scripture: Luke 15:11–32

Summary: A young man asked his father for his share of the family's wealth and left home to live a wild life. He spent all his money and had nothing left. Feeling very sorry, he decided to return home and ask his father for forgiveness.

When the young man returned, he was afraid of his father's anger. But his father was overjoyed to see him. He welcomed his son home with open arms.

Lesson: God's love gives us second chances.

Prayer: Thank You, Father for Your forgiving love. Amen.

Activity: Act the story of the Prodigal Son.

Day 10: Parable of the Money Lender
Scripture: Luke 7:41–43

Summary: A woman with a sinful past came to Jesus while He was eating at Simon the Pharisee's house. She wept at His feet, washed them with her tears, and anointed them with perfume. Simon was shocked. Jesus told a story about two people who owed money. The one who was forgiven more would love more. He said to Simon, "Her sins, which are many, are forgiven—for she loved much."

Lesson: We should love, forgive and not judge others so harshly.

Prayer: Jesus, teach us not to condemn. Amen.

Activity: Share the story with others.

Day 11: The Wise and Foolish Builders
Scripture: Matthew 7:24–27

Summary: A wise man built his house on a rock. A foolish man built his house on sand. When the rain came and the wind blew, the wise man's house stood strong, but the foolish man's house fell down.

Lesson: Build your life on Jesus' teachings.
Prayer: Lord, help us to build our lives on Your words. Amen.
Activity: Build towers with blocks on different surfaces.
Song: *My hope is built on nothing else, than Jesus blood and righteousness…*

Day 12: The Workers in the Vineyard
Scripture: Matthew 20:1–16

Summary: When we work, like doing our daily chores, we should work with our whole heart. Workers are hired at different times but paid the same wage. It is good to discuss wages/rewards we would get at the end if this is applicable. A worker is worthy of his wages and God who as a righteous judge pays us all for the work we do in His kingdom.

Lesson: God's grace is given to all.
Prayer: Thank You, God, for Your generous grace. Amen.
Activity: Do a chore and discuss fairness.

Day 13: The Two Sons
Scripture: Matthew 21:28–32

Summary: Two sons promised their father they would work in his vineyard. One son said no but later changed his mind and went. The other son said yes but didn't go. Jesus asked, "Which son did what his father wanted?" The answer showed that doing what you say you will do is more important than just saying it.

Lesson: Actions speak louder than words. Let us keep to our words when we say things.

Prayer: Jesus, help us to follow through on our commitments. Amen.

Activity: Draw 2 boys and discuss the story.

Day 14: The Talents
Scripture: Matthew 25:14–30

Summary: A master gives his servants different amounts of money to invest. Two servants worked hard and made more money. But one servant was scared and hid the money. When the man returned, he was happy with the hard-working servants and gave them more. But he was sad with the lazy servant and took his money away.

Lesson: Use the gifts God has given you. God does not want us to be lazy.
Prayer: Lord, help us to use our talents for Your glory. Amen.
Activity: Discuss and share your talents.

Day 15: The Ten Virgins
The Wise and Foolish Virgins
Scripture: Matthew 25:1–13

Summary: Ten virgins await the bridegroom, but only five are prepared. What made them wise?

Preparedness: The wise virgins brought extra oil for their lamps.

Responsibility: By bringing extra oil, they ensured that they would be able to fulfill their role in the wedding procession, regardless of any delays.

Faithfulness: They were dedicated to his arrival, no matter how long it took.

Lesson: Be prepared for Jesus' return.

Prayer: Jesus, help us to be ready for Your return. Amen.

Activity: Write something important you are waiting for in your journal.

Day 16: The Good Samaritan
Scripture: Luke 10:30–37

Summary: A man was wounded. The priest and others passed and did not care to help him. But a Samaritan, who was traveling, came where the man was; and when he saw him, he took pity on him. He went to him and bandaged his wounds, pouring on oil and wine. Then he put the man on his own donkey, brought him to an inn, took care of him and paid his bills.

Lesson: Love your neighbour as yourself.
Prayer: Jesus, help us to love others with Your love. Amen
Activity: Make a first aid kit.

Day 17: The Rich Fool
Scripture: Luke 12:16–21

Summary: A rich man had a great harvest. He thought, "I know! I'll build bigger barns to store all my wealth." But God said, "You foolish man! Tonight, your life will be taken from you. Then who will own all that you have gathered?" Remember that being rich isn't the most important thing in life. God wants us to be rich but we should not love wealth more than God.

Lesson: Don't be greedy; be rich towards God.

Prayer: Lord, teach us to value what really matters. Amen.

Activity: Draw a treasure chest with things that matter to God.

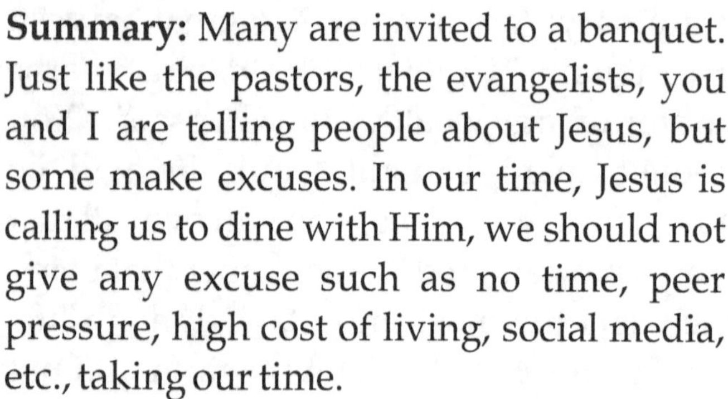

Day 18: The Great Banquet
Scripture: Luke 14:15–24

Summary: Many are invited to a banquet. Just like the pastors, the evangelists, you and I are telling people about Jesus, but some make excuses. In our time, Jesus is calling us to dine with Him, we should not give any excuse such as no time, peer pressure, high cost of living, social media, etc., taking our time.

Lesson: Be ready to accept God's invitation, while it is day and grace is available.

Prayer: Jesus, help us to accept and share Your invitation. Amen.

Activity: Watch a movie of how a party banquet e.g., birthday party was planned.

Day 19: The Parable of the Rich Man and Lazarus
Scripture: Luke 16:19-31

Summary: Jesus tells the story of a rich man and a poor man named Lazarus who lay at the rich man's gate, sick and ate what fell from the rich man's table. The rich man didn't know God. Both died, Lazarus went to Abraham's bosom, and the rich man ended up in torment in Hades.

Lesson: It teaches us to acknowledge God as we get rich and the importance of compassion.
Prayer: Lord, help me to show compassion to those in need.
Activity: Discuss ways to help the needy in your community.

Day 20: The Pharisee and the Tax Collector
Scripture: Luke 18:9–14

Summary: Two men went to the temple to pray. One man, a Pharisee, stood proudly and prayed out loud about how good he was. The other man, a tax collector, felt sorry for his sins and asked God for mercy. Jesus said that the humble tax collector was more pleasing to God than the proud Pharisee. God resists the proud and gives grace to the humble.
The man was sincere and repented.

Lesson: Be humble before God.
Prayer: Lord, help us to be humble and honest before You. Amen.
Activity: Role-play the prayers.

Day 21: The Fig Tree
Scripture: Luke 13:6–9

Summary: A man had a fig tree in his vineyard. Year after year, he hoped it would bear fruit, but it didn't. Finally, he said to the gardener, "Cut it down! Why should it use up the soil?" But the gardener asked for one more year to care for it. If it bore fruit, it could stay. If not, it would be cut down.

Lesson: God is patient and wants us to bear fruit.
Prayer: Jesus, help us to grow and bear fruit for You. Amen.
Activity: Draw a fruit tree.

Day 22: The Unforgiving Servant
Scripture: Matthew 18:21–35

Summary: A servant is forgiven a large debt but refuses to forgive a small one. In saying "Our Lord's prayer", Jesus taught us to pray and He said, "…Forgive us our sins as we forgive those who sin against us." That means God forgives us as we forgive others. If we do not forgive others, God will not forgive us.

Lesson: We ought to forgive others as God has forgiven us.

Prayer: Lord, help us to forgive others. Amen.

Activity: Discuss forgiveness and share experiences. Recite the Lord's prayer.

Day 23: The Parable of the Wheat and the Tares
Scripture: Matthew 13:24-30

Summary: A man sowed a good seed in his field, but while everyone slept, his enemy came and sowed weeds among the wheat. Both grew. The servants asked if they should pull up the weeds, but the owner said to let both grow together until the harvest.

Lesson: This parable teaches about the coexistence of good and evil in the world and the ultimate separation that will occur at the time of judgment.

Prayer: Lord, help us to grow in righteousness.

Activity: Discuss the importance of nurturing good qualities in our lives.

Day 24: The Sheep and the Goats
Scripture: Matthew 25:31–46

Summary: Once upon a time, Jesus told a story about a king who judged all the nations. He separated the good people from the bad. The good people were kind to others, like feeding the hungry. The bad people were selfish and didn't care about others. Jesus said that the good people would go to heaven, and the bad people would go to hell.

Lesson: It's important to be kind and helpful to others.

Prayer: Lord, help us to serve others and see You in them. Amen.

Activity: Make a list of ways to serve others.

Day 25: The Ten Minas
Scripture: Luke 19:11–27

Summary: A man gave ten servants ten coins each to invest. One servant buried his coin. The others used theirs to make more money. When the man returned, he praised the hard-working servants and punished the lazy one. We should use our talents and abilities to serve God.

Lesson: Use what God has given you wisely. Do not hide your talent. You can also use your gift to serve in church like ushering, singing, or playing instruments.

Prayer: Lord, help us to use Your gifts for Your glory. Amen.

Activity: Draw and decorate a coin.

Day 26: The Parable of the Persistent Widow
Scripture: Luke 18:2–8

Summary: There was a judge who didn't like helping people. A poor widow kept going to him, asking for help. The judge didn't want to listen. The widow didn't give up. She kept going back. Finally, the judge agreed to help her. Jesus said, "Even though the judge was unkind, he eventually listened because she was persistent."

Lesson: Never give up on praying, even when it feels like God isn't listening.

Prayer: God help me not to quit or give up on the things that matter in life.

Activity: Role-play the story with your toys.

Day 27: Review of the Wise and Foolish Virgins
Scripture: Matthew 25:1–13

Why were they wise? It is because they had extra oil.

We need to build extra skills as children. The extras that can differentiate you from other children include:

1. Salvation
2. The Holy Spirit
3. Skills like Resilience and Empathy
4. Positive Mindset
5. Learning skills like crafts, painting, playing musical instruments, athletic skills, making hair, making beads, sewing, etc.

Prayer: God help me to be wise, and to identify the skills that can help me to be different in my generation.

Action: What are the extra skills you need to learn to be better prepared as you grow? Enroll in them now.

Day 28: Review of the Parable of the Minas
Text: Luke 19:11-27

Let us look at this parable from budgeting and investment perspectives

Start by appreciating what you have. Life, health, and parts of your body.

Be grateful for what your parents can provide for you for now.

Use your talent well. It could be singing, dancing, recitation, drawing, or painting. The more you develop it, the more it blooms. Even if you don't have enough now, financial challenges can also help you develop discipline, patience, and foresight. When you have enough things like food and money leftovers, how can you save them?

Start today, and turn everyday moments into valuable financial lessons.

Day 29: Learning from the Parables
Scripture: Matthew 13:10–17

Jesus used parables to teach His Disciples Mention some of the parables and say which one is your favourite parable.

Reflection: What stood out for you in that parable and what did God use it to speak to you about in your own life?

Action: What actions from the parables you studied will you teach your classmates, siblings and friends? Humility, forgiveness, obedience, or being prepared?

Prayer: God, please help me to live daily in obedience to what you have taught me from this parable.

Day 30: Complete the puzzle below

The Prodigal Son Word Scramble

Unscramble each of the clue words. Take the letters that appear in the circle boxes and unscramble them to find the answer to the last phrase.

GRENUH

RVATLE

AFTEHR

EHOM

HOOLISF

Jesus teaches us

The Prodigal Son Word Scramble

Unscramble each of the clue words. Take the letters that appear in the circle boxes and unscramble them to find the answer to the last phrase.

GRENUH   H U N G E R

RVATLE   T R A V E L

AFTEHR   F A T H E R

EHOM   H O M E

HOOLISF   F O O L I S H

Jesus teaches us

T O   F O R G I V E

Notes

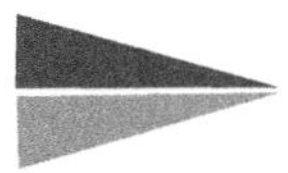 # Next Steps

Thank you for using this devotional guide for the past 6 months. I know you have grown in your knowledge of the Word of God and your relationship with Jesus. I trust that you will continue to put these words into practice, and as we go into July, I want to let you know that the second edition of the devotional, which spans from July to December, is available. Please get a copy and continue the adventure of our knowledge of Jesus as we cannot possibly get enough of the Word of God. May you continue to nurture the seed planted already. Remember that success needs maintenance, so don't say you have achieved it. Just like Apostle Paul said, "I forget what is behind and strain towards what is ahead." Brace up for another exciting time of learning at the feet of Jesus. God bless you.